Dictionary of

1000

Chinese Proverbs

Revised Edition

Dictionary of

1000

Chinese Proverbs

Revised Edition

Marjorie Lin
&
Schalk Leonard

HIPPOCRENE BOOKS, INC.
New York

For information, address:
HIPPOCRENE BOOKS, INC.
171 Madison Avenue
New York, NY 10016
www.hippocrenebooks.com

Library of Congress Cataloging-in-Publication Data

Dictionary of 1,000 Chinese proverbs / compiled and translated by Marjorie Lin and Schalk Leonard. -- Rev. ed.
    p. cm.
Text in English and Chinese.
"With new introduction by the authors."
Includes index.
ISBN 978-0-7818-1296-2 (pbk.)
ISBN 0-7818-1296-8 (pbk.)
1. Proverbs, Chinese. 2. English language--Dictionaries--Chinese.
3. Chinese language--Dictionaries--English. I. Lin, Marjorie. II. Leonard, Schalk. III. Title: Dictionary of one thousand Chinese proverbs.
PN6519.C5D53 2012
398.9'95103--dc23
                              2012036121

Introduction

The authors have selected and assembled in this volume one thousand of the most significant proverbs currently used in the Chinese language. Significance, as the central criterion for selection, includes frequency of popular usage, but also refers to the tendency of a given proverb to poignantly express traditional Chinese wisdom, beliefs, values, and aspirations. In this volume one will find proverbs expressing Taoist and Buddhist truths, Confucian rules of propriety, admonishments of the elderly, exhortations from parents, advice from teachers, and lessons for life learned from successive generations throughout history. The reader may discover, after a generous perusal of the Chinese proverbs contained herein, certain unique themes and features of Chinese life and thought. Among which, one may detect a strong preference for the particular over the general and the concrete over the abstract, generous use of symbolism, respect for the wisdom of the ancients, a persistent emphasis on the importance of study and learning, a tendency toward caution and frugality, inclinations toward social hierarchy, reliance on individual ethics, and a search for truth through examination of nature.

The main body of this volume contains proverb entries arranged in the following way: alphabetical arrangement based on the pinyin spelling of the first and, if necessary, succeeding terms in the proverb, with tone marks provided for the pinyin spelling entries; the simplified version of the characters in Chinese; the traditional version of the characters in Chinese; and, an English translation, and where possible, a corresponding English language proverb. The authors have attempted to translate each proverb as literally as possible, but in cases where this would lead to an unintelligible entry, a corresponding English-language statement of the meaning of the proverb is provided.

The authors have also provided an English key word index and a Chinese character concordance at the end of the volume. The English key word index contains an alphabetical listing of key English language terms used in the translation of each proverb, while the Chinese character concordance contains the key Chinese language character terms in the proverbs, arranged based on the alphabetical pinyin spelling of the characters. Numbers following the English key words and Chinese character concordance terms indicate the page on which the proverb containing that key word or character can be located in the volume.

The pinyin system of romanization is used throughout the volume. This system was established in the People's Republic of China in the 1950s and has gained increasing acceptance throughout the world as a coherent and useful system of romanization for Chinese character terms.

In this volume, the Mandarin dialect of the Chinese language is used exclusively. Chinese Mandarin is said to be the oldest continuously spoken language in the world, it claims more speakers than any other language in the world, and it is by far the most widely used and understood dialect of Chinese.

A

aī mò dà yú xīn sǐ

哀莫大于心死。

哀莫大於心死。

There is no greater sorrow than a cold heart.

ài ér dāng xùn zǐ

爱儿当训子。

愛兒當訓子。

If you love your child, you should discipline your child.

àn rén kǒu zuò fàn, liáng shēn tǐ cái yī

按人口做饭, 量身体裁衣。

按人口做飯, 量身體裁衣。

Cook your meal based on the number of people, and cut your cloth according to your size.

Suit the measure to the condition.

B

bái rì bú zuò kuī xīn shì, bàn yè bú pà guǐ qiāo mén

白日不做亏心事, 半夜不怕鬼敲门。

白日不做虧心事, 半夜不怕鬼敲門。

One with a clear conscience is not jumpy when there is a midnight knock on the door.

bǎi chuān guī hǎi

百川归海。

百川歸海。

All rivers return to the sea.

All roads lead to Rome.

bǎi lǐ bù tóng fēng

百里不同风。

百里不同風。

Every one hundred miles you'll find different customs.

bǎi mì bì yǒu yì shū

百密必有一疏。

百密必有一疏。

You can't cover every base.

bǎi rì lián yīn yǔ, zǒng yǒu yì zhāo qíng

百日连阴雨，总有一朝晴。

百日連陰雨，總有一朝晴。

A long spell of clouds and rain will be followed by a sunny day.

bǎi wén bù rú yí jiàn

百闻不如一见。

百聞不如一見。

Better to see once than to hear one hundred times.

bǎi yàng què ér bǎi yàng yīn

百样雀儿百样音。

百樣雀兒百樣音。

One hundred different sparrows make one hundred different sounds.

bǎo hàn bù zhī è hàn jī

饱汉不知饿汉饥。

飽漢不知餓漢飢。

The well-fed do not know how the starving suffer.

bào sǐ liú pí, rén sǐ liú míng

豹死留皮，人死留名。

豹死留皮，人死留名。

The leopard dies but leaves his skin, and a man dies but leaves his reputation.

bēi xǐ wéi lín

悲喜为邻。

悲喜為鄰。

Happiness and sorrow are neighbors.

bèi quǎn suǒ fèi zhě, wèi bì jiē dào qiè

被犬所吠者, 未必皆盗窃。

被犬所吠者, 未必皆盜竊。

Not everyone the dog barks at is a thief.

biān xué biān wèn, cái yǒu xué wèn

边学边问, 才有学问。

邊學邊問, 才有學問。

Study and inquiry are the path to knowledge.

biǎn dàn méi zā, liǎng tóu dǎ tā

扁担没扎, 两头打塌。

扁擔沒扎, 兩頭打塌。

When the carrying pole is not secured at both ends, the load will slip off.

biàn dì jiē huáng jīn, zhuān děng qín kǔ rén

遍地皆黄金, 专等勤苦人。

遍地皆黄金, 專等勤苦人。

There is gold everywhere waiting to be seized by the industrious.

bié zì zhǎo má fán

别自找麻烦。

別自找麻煩。

Don't go looking for trouble.

Let sleeping dogs lie.

bīng bú yàn zhà

兵不厌诈。

兵不厭詐。

Deception is fine in war.

All is fair in war.

bīng bù lí zhèn, hǔ bù lí shān

兵不离阵, 虎不离山。

兵不離陣, 虎不離山。

Soldiers do not stray from their posts, and tigers do not stray from the mountain.

bīng dòng sān chǐ, fēi yí rì zhī hán

冰冻三尺, 非一日之寒。

冰凍三尺, 非一日之寒。

It takes more than one cold day for a river to freeze over three feet thick.

Significant problems do not arise overnight.

bīng guì jīng, bú guì duō

兵贵精, 不贵多。

兵貴精, 不貴多。

Troops are valued for their quality, not their quantity.

bīng guì shén sù, rén guì sī suǒ

兵贵神速, 人贵思索。

兵貴神速, 人貴思索。

Troops are valued for their speed as men are valued for their minds.

bīng suí jiàng xiàng cǎo suí fēng

兵随将相草随风。

兵隨將相草隨風。

Troops follow their general as grass sways in the direction of the wind.

bìng cóng kǒu rù, huò cóng kǒu chū

病从口入, 祸从口出。

病從口入, 禍從口出。

The mouth is the entry point of disease and the departure point of misfortune.

bìng hǎo bú xiè yī, xià cì méi rén yī

病好不谢医, 下次没人医。

病好不謝醫, 下次沒人醫。

Thank the doctor when you recover, or you won't find a doctor the next time you are ill.

bìng jí luàn tóu yī

病急乱投医。

病急亂投醫。

When critically ill, one will try any doctor.
The desperate will try anything.

bó lì duō xiāo shēng yì hǎo

薄利多销生意好。

薄利多銷生意好。

Business will boom when profits are slashed to drive sales.

bú huì shāo xiāng dé zuì shén, bú huì jiǎng huà dé zuì rén

不会烧香得罪神, 不会讲话得罪人。

不會燒香得罪神, 不會講話得罪人。

If you don't know how to pray, you offend the gods; if you don't know how to speak, you offend others.

bú pà làng tóu gāo, jiù pà jiǎng bù qí

不怕浪头高, 就怕桨不齐。

不怕浪頭高, 就怕槳不齊。

Be more concerned about the inability to row in unison than the high waves.

bú pà lù cháng, zhǐ pà zhì duǎn

不怕路长, 只怕志短。

不怕路長, 只怕志短。

A long journey will not deter one with high aspirations.

bú pà rén bù qǐng, jiù pà yì bù jīng

不怕人不请, 就怕艺不精。

不怕人不請, 就怕藝不精。

Be more concerned about your lack of skill than the absence of an employer.

bú pà rén lǎo, zhǐ pà xīn lǎo

不怕人老, 只怕心老。

不怕人老, 只怕心老。

Fear not old age but only an old heart.

bú pà shēng huài mìng, jiù pà shēng huài bìng

不怕生坏命, 就怕生坏病。

不怕生壞命, 就怕生壞病。

Be more concerned about bad illness than about bad fate.

bú pà shì qíng nán, jiù pà bú nài fán

不怕事情难, 就怕不耐烦。

不怕事情難, 就怕不耐煩。

No task is too difficult if you are patient.

bú pà xiāng guì kōng, zhǐ yào yǒu ge hǎo lǎo gōng

不怕箱柜空, 只要有个好老公。

不怕箱櫃空, 只要有個好老公。

With a good husband, there is no concern about an empty wardrobe.

bú pà xué bù chéng, jiù pà xīn bù chéng

不怕学不成, 就怕心不诚。

不怕學不成, 就怕心不誠。

Be more concerned about the sincerity of your effort than about your ability to learn.

bú pà zhī duǎn, jiù pà zhì duǎn

不怕知短, 就怕志短。

不怕知短, 就怕志短。

Be more concerned about lofty aspirations than limited knowledge.

bú rù hǔ xuè, yān dé hǔ zǐ

不入虎穴, 焉得虎子。

不入虎穴, 焉得虎子。

To capture a tiger cub, you must enter the tiger's lair. Nothing ventured, nothing gained.

bú shàng dàng, bù chéng háng jiā

不上当, 不成行家。

不上當, 不成行家。

If you have never been fooled, you'll never become an expert.

bú shàng gāo shān, bù xiǎn píng dì

不上高山, 不显平地。

不上高山, 不顯平地。

If you don't climb a high mountain, you won't see the valley.

bú shì lú shān zhēn miàn mù, zhǐ yuán shēn zài cǐ shān zhōng

不识庐山真面目, 只缘身在此山中。

不識廬山真面目, 只緣身在此山中。

When I am standing on Mt. Lu, I do not see the true face of Mt. Lu.

bú shì yuān jiā bú jù tóu

不是冤家不聚头。

不是冤家不聚頭。

Those with mutual ties will end up together.

bú wèi bù zhī ér xiū, yào wèi bù xué ér kuì

不为不知而羞, 要为不学而愧。

不為不知而羞, 要為不學而愧。

Be ashamed of not learning, rather than of not knowing.

bú xì jiáo, bù zhī wèi

不细嚼, 不知味。

不細嚼, 不知味。

You can't savor the flavor if you don't chew thoroughly.

bú yào kàn jiǎo zěn me yàng, yào kàn zǒu lù zhèng bú zhèng

不要看脚怎么样, 要看走路正不正。

不要看腳怎么樣, 要看走路正不正。

Pay attention to how someone walks rather than to how his legs look.

Judge a person by how he conducts himself rather than how he looks.

bǔ lòu chèn qíng tiān, dú shū chèn nián qīng

补露趁晴天, 读书趁年轻。

補露趁晴天, 讀書趁年輕。

Fix the roof when the skies are clear; acquire knowledge while you are still young.

bù cháng huáng lián kǔ, nǎ zhī fēng mì tián

不尝黄莲苦, 哪知蜂蜜甜。

不嚐黃蓮苦, 哪知蜂蜜甜。

One cannot know sweet without tasting bitter.

bù chī fàn zé jī, bù dú shū zé yú

不吃饭则饥, 不读书则愚。

不吃飯則飢, 不讀書則愚。

Eat to ward off starvation and study to ward off ignorance.

bù dǎ bù chéng qì

不打不成器。

不打不成器。

Spare the rod and spoil the child.

bù dǎ bù xiāng shì

不打不相识。

不打不相識。

No discord, no concord.

bù dāng jiā, bù zhī chái mǐ guì;
bù shēng zǐ, bù zhī fù mǔ ēn

不当家, 不知柴米贵;不生子, 不知父母恩。

不當家, 不知柴米貴;不生子, 不知父母恩。

You don't know the price of firewood and rice until you've managed a household; you don't know the love of a parent until you've had children of your own.

bù dǔ shì yíng qián

不赌是赢钱。

不賭是贏錢。

One wins by not gambling.

bù jīng dōng hán, nǎ zhī chūn nuǎn

不经冬寒, 哪知春暖。

不經冬寒, 哪知春暖。

You must live through winter to appreciate the warmth of spring.

bù jīng yí shì, bù zhǎng yí zhì

不经一事, 不长一智。

不經一事, 不長一智。

You can't gain knowledge without experience.

bù juǎn kù jiǎo bú guò hé, bù mō dǐ xì bù kāi qiāng

不卷裤脚不过河, 不摸底细不开腔。

不捲褲腳不過河, 不摸底細不開腔。

Don't cross the river without first rolling up your pant legs; don't speak without first knowing what you are talking about.

bù mō chèng gǎn, bù zhī tuó zhòng

不摸秤杆, 不知砣重。

不摸秤桿, 不知砣重。

You must shoulder a load to appreciate its weight.

bù sī jiǎo de rén, bǔ bú dào yú

不湿脚的人，补不到鱼。

不濕腳的人，補不到魚。

Those who don't get their feet wet don't catch fish.

bù tān cái, huò bù lái

不贪财，祸不来。

不貪財，禍不來。

Those who are not greedy do not court disasters.

bù tiāo dàn zi bù zhī zhòng, bù zǒu yuǎn lù bù zhī yuǎn

不挑担子不知重，不走远路不知远。

不挑擔子不知重，不走遠路不知遠。

You can't appreciate the weight of a load until you shoulder it; you can't appreciate the length of a road until you travel it.

bù tīng lǎo rén yán, chī kuī zài yǎn qián

不听老人言，吃亏在眼前。

不聽老人言，吃虧在眼前。

If you ignore the advice of elders, you will quickly come to grief.

bù yǐ chéng bài lùn yīng xióng

不以成败论英雄。

不以成敗論英雄。

Don't judge a hero by whether he wins or loses.

bù zhī jiù wèn, bù néng zé xué

不知就问，不能则学。

不知就問，不能則學。

You should ask if you don't know, and you should study if you don't know how.

C

cái duō bú lòu, yì gāo bù xiǎn;
ài lòu ài xiǎn, bì yǒu fēng xiǎn

财多不露, 艺高不显;爱露爱显, 必有风险。

財多不露, 藝高不顯;愛露愛顯, 必有風險。

Don't parade your riches or talent; those who show off court danger.

cái duō lèi shēn, yù duō shāng shēn

财多累身, 欲多伤身

財多累身, 慾多傷身。

Excess riches tire the body and excess desire harms the soul.

cái duō zhāo zéi, rén jùn zhāo xié

财多招贼, 人俊招邪。

財多招賊, 人俊招邪。

Wealth attracts thieves as beauty attracts evil.

cāo xīn yì lǎo

操心易老。

操心易老。

Worry causes aging.

chā zhī háo lǐ, miù yǐ qiān lǐ

差之毫厘，谬以千里。

差之毫厘，謬以千里。

A tiny error may lead one far astray.

chāi dōng qiáng, bǔ xī qiáng, jié guǒ hái shì zhù pò fáng

拆东墙，补西墙，结果还是住破房。

拆東牆，補西牆，結果還是住破房。

If you tear down the east wall to fix the west wall, you still have a broken-down house.

**cháng jiāng hòu làng tuī qián làng,
yí dài gèng bǐ yí dài qiáng**

长江后浪推前浪，一代更比一代强。

長江後浪推前浪，一代更比一代強。

As one wave pushes the next, new generations transcend previous ones.

cháng kāi chuāng, bǎo jiàn kāng

常开窗，保健康。

常開窗，保健康。

Fresh air is good for the health.

cháng mà bù jīng, cháng dǎ bù líng

常骂不惊，常打不灵。

常罵不驚，常打不靈。

Excessive scoldings and beatings lose their intended effect.

cháng shuō kǒu lǐ shùn, cháng zuò shǒu bú bèn

常说口里顺, 常做手不笨。

常說口裡順, 常做手不笨。

You will speak naturally if you say it often, and you won't be clumsy if you do it often.

Practice makes perfect.

cháng sī jǐ guò, miǎn yú zhāo huò

常思己过, 免于招祸。

常思己過, 免於招禍。

Ponder your faults and you will avoid misfortune.

cháng wèn lù, bù mí lù

常问路, 不迷路。

常問路, 不迷路。

You won't get lost if you frequently ask for directions.

chē dào shān qián bì yǒu lù

车到山前必有路。

車到山前必有路。

The cart will find its way around the hill when it gets there.

Things will work out in time.

chē yǒu chē dào, mǎ yǒu mǎ lù

车有车道, 马有马路。

車有車道, 馬有馬路。

There are lanes for vehicles and there are roads for horses.

chéng gōng shì sān fēn tiān cái qī fēn nǔ lì

成功是三分天才七分努力。

成功是三分天才七分努力。

Success is three parts genius and seven parts hard work.

chéng jiàn bù kě yǒu, dìng jiàn bù kě wú

成见不可有, 定见不可无。

成見不可有, 定見不可無。

One should maintain firm views without becoming prejudiced.

chèng néng chēng qīng zhòng, huà néng liáng rén xīn

秤能称轻重, 话能量人心。

秤能稱輕重, 話能量人心。

As scales measure weight, words gauge feelings.

chī de kǔ zhōng kǔ, fāng wéi rén shàng rén

吃得苦中苦, 方为人上人。

吃得苦中苦, 方為人上人。

Only those who can withstand the utmost hardship can rise in society.

chī kuī jiù shì zhàn pián yí

吃亏就是占便宜。

吃虧就是佔便宜。

The lesson you learn when you are taken advantage of puts you at an advantage.

chī yí qiàn, zhǎng yí zhì

吃一堑, 长一智。

吃一塹, 長一智。

A fall in the pit, a gain in your wit.

chī yì huí kuī, xué yì huí guāi

吃一回亏, 学一回乖。

吃一回虧, 學一回乖。

Those who are taken advantage of become wiser for it.

chí lǐ wú yú xiā wéi dà, shān zhōng wú hǔ hóu wéi wáng

池里无鱼虾为大, 山中无虎猴为王。

池裡無魚蝦為大, 山中無虎猴為王。

When there are no fish in the pond, the shrimp are in charge; when there are no tigers on the mountain, the monkey is king.

chǒu fù jiā zhōng bǎo

丑妇家中宝。

醜婦家中寶。

The ugly housewife is a treasure at home.

chǒu rén ài dài huā

丑人爱戴花。

醜人愛戴花。

Ugly people like gaudy dress.
The inferior crave attention.

chǒu rén ài zuò guài
丑人爱作怪。
醜人愛作怪。
Ugly people like to do outrageous things.
The inferior love to be outlandish.

chū mén kàn tiān sè, mǎi mài kàn háng qíng
出门看天色, 买卖看行情。
出門看天色, 買賣看行情。
When you leave the house, check the weather; when you do
business, check the market.

chū mén wèn lù, rù xiāng wèn sú
出门问路, 入乡问俗。
出門問路, 入鄉問俗。
Ask for directions when you are out and about, and make
inquiries about customs when you visit a town.

chū shēng zhī dǔ bú wèi hǔ
初生之犊不畏虎。
初生之犢不畏虎。
New-born calves have no fear of tigers.

chú zi duō pàng zi
厨子多胖子。
廚子多胖子。
Cooks are generally plump.

chǔ jūn zi yì, chǔ xiǎo rén nán

处君子易，处小人难。

處君子易，處小人難。

It's easy to get along with a gentleman, but not with a
scoundrel.

chuán dà chī shuǐ shēn

船大吃水深。

船大吃水深。

Large boats have a deep draft.

chuán dào jiāng xīn bǔ lòu chí

船到江心补漏迟。

船到江心補漏遲。

When the boat is in mid-stream, it's too late to plug the leak.

chuán dào qiáo tóu zì rán zhí

船到桥头自然直。

船到橋頭自然直。

Everything will work out in the end.

chuán kào duò, fán kào fēng, lì jiàn hái yào kào qiáng gōng

船靠舵，帆靠风，利箭还要靠强弓。

船靠舵，帆靠风，利箭还要靠强弓。

Boats rely on rudders, sails rely on wind, and sharp arrows
still need strong bows.

chuǎng huò róng yì, xiāo zāi nán

闯祸容易，消灾难。

闖禍容易，消災難。

It is easy to court trouble, but hard to avert it.

chuàng yè nán, shǒu chéng gèng nán

创业难，守成更难。

創業難，守成更難。

It is hard to start an undertaking, but it is even harder to maintain it.

chūn gēng bù hǎo hài yì nián, jiāo zǐ bù hǎo hài yì shēng

春耕不好害一年，教子不好害一生。

春耕不好害一年，教子不好害一生。

One will suffer the whole year for not ploughing well in the spring, while one will suffer for life for not educating the children well.

chūn yǔ guì rú yóu

春雨贵如油

春雨貴如油

Spring rain is as precious as oil.

cí bù zhǎng bīng, yì bù zhǎng cái

慈不掌兵，义不掌财。

慈不掌兵，義不掌財。

The merciful do not engage in war, and the righteous do not engage in financial business.

cōng míng bǎo yì rén, fù guì bǎo yì jiā

聪明保一人，富贵保一家。

聰明保一人，富貴保一家。

Cleverness provides for the individual, fortune provides for the whole family.

cōng míng fǎn bèi cōng míng wù

聪明反被聪明误。

聰明反被聰明誤。

Clever people may be victims of their own cleverness.

cōng míng rén yě huì zuò shǎ shì

聪明人也会做傻事。

聰明人也會做傻事。

Smart people also do stupid things.

cóng shàn rú dēng, cóng è rú bēng

从善如登，从恶如崩。

從善如登，從惡如崩。

Pursuit of the good is like climbing, but pursuit of evil is like collapsing.

cū fàn yǎng rén, cū huó yǎng shēn

粗饭养人，粗活养身。

粗飯養人，粗活養身。

Simple food nurtures the people, and hard work nurtures the health.

cù shì chén de suān

醋是陈的酸。

醋是陳的酸。

Vinegar grows more pungent with age.

D

dǎ gǒu kàn zhǔ rén

打狗看主人。

打狗看主人。

Know who the master is before you beat his dog.

dǎ le sān nián guān sī, dāng de bàn ge lǜ shī

打了三年官司, 当得半个律师。

打了三年官司, 當得半個律師。

Pursue a lawsuit for three years and you'll know almost as much as a lawyer.

dǎ rén yì quán, fáng rén yì jiǎo

打人一拳, 防人一脚。

打人一拳, 防人一腳。

If you punch someone, watch out for his kick.

dǎ shì téng, mà shì ài

打是疼, 骂是爱。

打是疼, 罵是愛。

Discipline springs from love.

dǎ tiě xiān děi běn shēn yìng
打铁先得本身硬。

打鐵先得本身硬。

It takes a tough man to forge iron.
One must be ideologically sound and professionally competent to do arduous tasks.

dǎ tiě yào chèn rè
打铁要趁热。

打鐵要趁熱。

Strike while the iron is hot.

dà fù yóu tiān, xiǎo fù yóu jiǎn
大富由天, 小富由俭。

大富由天, 小富由儉。

Great wealth is determined by heaven, but moderate wealth comes from being thrifty.

dà gǒu pá qiáng, xiáo gǒu kàn yàng
大狗爬墙, 小狗看样。

大狗爬牆, 小狗看樣。

Big dogs climb the wall, and small dogs follow suit.
Monkey see, monkey do.

dà jī bù shí xì mǐ
大鸡不食细米。

大雞不食細米。

Large hens don't eat tiny grains of rice.

dà lù yǒu qiān tiáo, zhēn lǐ zhǐ yì tiáo

大路有千条, 真理只一条。

大路有千條, 真理只一條。

There are one thousand paths, but only one true path.

dà nàn bù sǐ, bì yǒu hòu fú

大难不死, 必有后福。

大難不死, 必有後福。

Those who survive a catastrophe are bound to have good fortune later.

dà shù yě yǒu gū zhī

大树也有枯枝。

大樹也有枯枝。

Even large trees have dry branches.

dà zhàng fū néng qū néng shēn

大丈夫能屈能伸。

大丈夫能屈能伸。

The real man is one who knows when to yield and when to stand firm.

dà zhì ruò yú

大智若愚。

大智若愚。

A man of great wisdom often appears slow-witted.
Still waters run deep.

dān sī bù chéng xiàn

单丝不成线。

單絲不成線。

A single strand of silk will not make a thread.

dān xián bù chéng yīn

单弦不成音。

單弦不成音。

You can't make music on a single string.

dǎn xiǎo zuò bù dé jiāng jūn

胆小做不得将军。

膽小做不得將軍。

The timid cannot serve as generals.

dāng jiā cái zhī chái mǐ guì, chū mén cái xiǎo lù nán xíng

当家才知柴米贵, 出门才晓路难行。

當家才知柴米貴, 出門才曉路難行。

Manage a household and you'll know the cost of firewood and rice; take a trip and you'll realize the difficulty of the journey.

dāng jú zhě mí, páng guān zhě qīng

当局者迷, 旁观者清。

當局者迷, 旁觀者清。

Outsiders see more clearly than insiders.

dāo qiāng bú rèn rén

刀枪不认人。

刀槍不認人。

Weapons make no distinctions among men.

dāo shāng yì zhì, kǒu shāng nán yī

刀伤易治，口伤难医。

刀傷易治，口傷難醫。

It is easy to treat the cut of a blade, but it is hard to treat the cut of words.

dào bù tóng, bù xiāng wéi móu

道不同，不相为谋。

道不同，不相為謀。

People who follow different paths do not consult with one other.

dào chù bú yòng qián, chù chù ruǒ rén xián

到处不用钱，处处惹人嫌。

到處不用錢，處處惹人嫌。

If you don't spend your money, you won't be welcome anywhere.

dào shén me miào, shāo shén me xiāng

到什么庙，烧什么香。

到甚麼廟，燒甚麼香。

Burn the right incense in the right temple.

When in Rome, do as the Romans do.

dé bù gū, bì yǒu lín

德不孤, 必有邻。

德不孤, 必有鄰。

Persons of high moral character will never be lonely and will always find good company.

dé bù zú xǐ, shī bù zú yōu

得不足喜, 失不足忧。

得不足喜, 失不足憂。

One should not be happy about gain or despondent about loss.

dé dào duō zhù, shī dào guǎ zhù

得道多助, 失道寡助。

得道多助, 失道寡助。

A just cause will enjoy wide support while an unjust cause will find little support.

dé ráo rén chù qiě ráo rén

得饶人处且饶人。

得饒人處且饒人。

Pardon others when you can.

dī shuǐ chuān shí

滴水穿石。

滴水穿石。

Constant dripping wears away the stone.

dōng bù jié yuē, chūn yào chóu;
xià bù láo dòng, qiū wú shōu

冬不节约, 春要愁；夏不劳动, 秋无收。

冬不節約, 春要愁；夏不勞動, 秋無收。

Be thrifty in the winter or you'll have worries in the spring; be industrious in the summer, or you'll have no harvest in the fall.

dōng jiā bú bài luò, xī jiā bù fā dá

东家不败落, 西家不发达。

東家不敗落, 西家不發達。

If Peter does not fail, Paul does not prosper. For every winner there is a loser.

dú mù bù chéng lín

独木不成林。

獨木不成林。

A single tree does not a forest make.

dú yuè lè, bù rú zhòng yuè lè

独乐乐, 不如众乐乐。

獨樂樂, 不如眾樂樂。

Music is best enjoyed with others.

dú zhuān bù chéng qiáng, dú huā bú shì chūn

独砖不成墙, 独花不是春。

獨磚不成牆, 獨花不是春。

A single brick does not make a wall, and a single flower does not make it spring.

duān rén jiā wǎn, fú rén jiā guǎn
端人家碗，服人家管。

端人家碗，服人家管。

When you work for another, submit to his supervision.

duì zhèng xià yào, yào dào bìng chú
对症下药，药到病除。

對症下藥，藥到病除。

The right medicine for the condition will take effect
immediately.

duō chī wú zī wèi, duō huà bù zhí qián
多吃无滋味，多话不值钱。

多吃無滋味，多話不值錢。

A glut of food is tasteless, and a glut of words is worthless.

duō nián xí fù áo chéng pó
多年媳妇熬成婆

多年媳婦熬成婆

Those who persist through hard times will find relief.

duō shēn de gēn jī, zhú duō gāo de qiáng
多深的根基，筑多高的墙。

多深的根基，築多高的牆。

The depth of the foundation determines the height of the
wall.

duō xíng bú yì bì zì bì

多行不义必自毙。

多行不義必自斃。

He who persists in bad deeds will come to a bad end.

duō yán ruǒ huò

多言惹祸。

多言惹禍。

The less said, the sooner mended.

E

è bù jī, bù zú yǐ sàng shēn

恶不积, 不足以丧身。

惡不積, 不足以喪身。

If you don't do bad deeds, you will not harm yourself.

è rén xiān gào zhuàng

恶人先告状。

惡人先告狀。

The guilty party always lodge a complaint first.

ér bù xián mǔ chǒu, gǒu bù xián zhǔ pín

儿不嫌母丑, 狗不嫌主贫。

兒不嫌母醜, 狗不嫌主貧。

A child will never desert his mother though she may be homely; a dog will never forsake its master though he may be poor.

ér dà bù yóu yé, nǚ dà bù yóu niáng

儿大不由爷, 女大不由娘。

兒大不由爺, 女大不由娘。

When boys grow up, they are beyond the father's control; when girls grow up, they are beyond the mother's control.

ér xíng qiān lǐ mǔ dān yōu

儿行千里母担忧。

兒行千里母擔憂。

When the child takes a trip, the mother will worry.

ěr wén wéi xū, yǎn jiàn wéi shí

耳闻为虚，眼见为实。

耳聞為虛，眼見為實。

What you hear may be false, but what you see is true.

F

fán nǎo bù xún rén, rén zì xún fán nǎo

烦恼不寻人, 人自寻烦恼。

煩惱不尋人, 人自尋煩惱。

Worry doesn't seek out people, but people find it on their own.

fán shì qǐ tóu nán, zuò le jiù bù nán

凡是起头难, 做了就不难。

凡是起頭難, 做了就不難。

Everything is hard at the beginning but gets easier once underway.

fán shì yù zé lì, bú yù zé fèi

凡事预则立, 不预则废。

凡事預則立, 不預則廢。

Come prepared and succeed, come unprepared and fail.

fàn hòu bǎi bù zǒu, huó dào jiǔ shí jiǔ

饭后百步走, 活到九十九。

飯後百步走, 活到九十九。

A good stroll after a meal makes for a long life.

fàn mò bù jiǎo biàn tūn, huà mò bù xiǎng jiù shuō

饭莫不嚼便吞, 话莫不想就说。

飯莫不嚼便吞, 話莫不想就說。

Do not swallow your food without chewing, and do not speak without thinking.

fāng huà nán rù yuán ěr duō

方话难入圆耳朵。

方話難入圓耳朵。

Square words won't fit into a round ear.
You can't please everyone.

fàng cháng xiàn, diào dà yú

放长线, 钓大鱼。

放長線, 釣大魚。

Throw a long line to catch a big fish.
Adopt long-term measures to achieve major success.

fàng xià tú dāo, lì dì chéng fó

放下屠刀, 立地成佛。

放下屠刀, 立地成佛。

A butcher becomes a Buddha the moment he drops his cleaver.
A wrongdoer may become a man of virtue once he stops doing bad deeds.

féi shuǐ bú luò wài rén tián

肥水不落外人田。

肥水不落外人田。

Every man diverts water to his own field.

Everyone serves his own self-interests.

fēng nián jiǎn, zāi nián zú

丰年俭, 灾年足。

豐年儉, 災年足。

Be thrifty in good times to survive in bad times.

fēng shōu méi yǒu qiǎo, duō chú jǐ biàn cǎo

丰收没有巧, 多除几遍草。

豐收沒有巧, 多除幾遍草。

There's no trick to a bountiful harvest - simply work your hoe and weed over and over.

féng rén zhǐ shuō sān fēn huà

逢人只说三分话。

逢人只說三分話。

Maintain your reserve when talking with others.

fū chàng fù suí

夫唱妇随。

夫唱婦隨。

The husband sings a song and the wife sings along.

fū qī chǎo zuǐ bú jì chóu

夫妻吵嘴不记仇。

夫妻吵嘴不記仇。

Quarreling spouses do not hold grudges.

fū qī hé, jiā wù xīng; fū qī bù hé, shuì bù níng

夫妻和，家务兴；夫妻不合，睡不宁。

夫妻和，家務興；夫妻不合，睡不寧。

When a couple gets along, the home prospers; when a couple fights, not even a night's sleep can be had.

fú wú shuāng zhì

福无双至。

福無雙至。

Blessings never come in pairs.

fǔ mù bù kě wéi zhù, bēi rén bù kě wéi zhǔ

腐木不可为柱，卑人不可为主。

腐木不可為柱，卑人不可為主。

Rotten wood cannot be used for pillars, and petty and low people cannot serve as leaders.

fù cháo zhī xià wú wán luǎn

覆巢之下无完卵。

覆巢之下無完卵。

When the nest is overturned, all of the eggs will be broken.

fù guì hǎo, bù rú ér sūn hǎo

富贵好, 不如儿孙好。

富貴好, 不如兒孫好。

It is good to be rich, but even better to have good children.

fù shuǐ nán shōu

覆水难收。

覆水難收。

Spilt water cannot be retrieved.
It is no use crying over spilt milk.

G

gài de zhù huǒ, cáng bú zhù yān

盖得住火, 藏不住烟。

蓋得住火, 藏不住煙。

You can cover up fire, but you can't hide smoke.

gāng mù yì zhé, qiáng gōng yì duàn

刚木易折, 强弓易断。

剛木易折, 強弓易斷。

Hard wood and strong bows break easily.

gé céng dù pí, gé chóng shān

隔层肚皮, 隔重山。

隔層肚皮, 隔重山。

A belly apart, mountains apart.

You can never really fathom the mind of another.

gé qiáng yǒu ěr

隔墙有耳。

隔牆有耳。

Walls have ears.

gè rén zì sǎo mén qián xuě, mò guǎn tā rén wǎ shàng shuāng

各人自扫门前雪, 莫管他人瓦上霜。

各人自掃門前雪, 莫管他人瓦上霜。

Sweep the snow on your own doorstep and don't mind the frost on your neighbor's roof.

Mind your own business.

gēn shén me rén, xué shén me yàng;
gēn zhe tǔ fū, xué bù chéng pí jiàng

跟甚么人, 学甚么样; 跟着屠夫, 学不成皮匠。

跟甚麼人, 學甚麼樣; 跟著屠夫, 學不成皮匠。

Our learning is dictated by our teacher; if we study with a butcher, we won't become a cobbler.

gōng dào zì rán chéng

功到自然成。

功到自然成。

Constant effort yields certain success.

gōng lǐ shèng qiáng quán

公理胜强权。

公理勝強權。

Truth is more powerful than force.

gōng shuō gōng yǒu lǐ, pó shuó pó yǒu lǐ

公说公有理, 婆说婆有理。

公說公有理, 婆說婆有理。

Husband and wife both say they are right.

There are two sides to every issue.

gōng yù shàn qí shì, bì xiān lì qí qì

工欲善其事, 必先利其器。

工欲善其事, 必先利其器。

The worker must first sharpen his tools if he is to do his work well.

gǒu jí tiào qiáng, rén jí zào fǎn

狗急跳墙, 人急造反。

狗急跳墙, 人急造反。

The cornered dog will vault over a wall, and the desperate man will rebel.

gǒu yǎn kàn rén dī, rén qióng gǒu yě qī

狗眼看人低, 人穷狗也欺。

狗眼看人低, 人窮狗也欺。

Dogs regard men as inferior, and when a man is poor, the dog will bully him.

gǒu zuǐ tǔ bù chū xiàng yá

狗嘴吐不出象牙。

狗嘴吐不出象牙。

A dog's mouth will not produce ivory.
A filthy mouth will not utter decent language.

gǔ bù qiāo bù xiǎng, lǐ bú biàn bù míng

鼓不敲不响, 理不辩不明。

鼓不敲不響, 理不辯不明。

The drum will not make a sound until it is struck, and the truth will not become evident until it is debated.

gǔ kōng zé shēng gāo, rén kuáng zé huà dà

鼓空则声高，人狂则话大。

鼓空則聲高，人狂則話大。

Empty drums make a loud noise, and arrogant men make loud boasts.

gù yǒu shèng xīn zhī

故友胜新知。

故友勝新知。

Old friends are better than new acquaintances.

guǎ fù mén qián shì fēi duō

寡妇门前是非多。

寡婦門前是非多。

There are many disputes in front of the widow's door.

guǎ jiǔ nán hē, guǎ fù nán áo

寡酒难喝，寡妇难熬。

寡酒難喝，寡婦難熬。

It's no fun to drink alone, and it's hard being a widow.

guān xiǎo bèi rén qī, shù lǎo fēng chuī dǎo

官小被人欺，树老风吹倒。

官小被人欺，樹老風吹倒。

The minor official will be bullied by the people, as the old tree will be blown down by the wind.

guǎn xián shì, luò bú shì

管闲事，落不是。

管閒事，落不是。

Mind the business of others and you will be blamed in the end.

guāng tóu bù yí dìng shì hé shàng

光头不一定是和尚。

光頭不一定是和尚。

Not every bald head belongs to a monk.

guāng yīn róng yì guò, suì yuè mò cuō tuó

光阴容易过，岁月莫蹉跎。

光陰容易過，歲月莫蹉跎。

Time passes quickly, so don't waste it.
Carpe diem.

guāng yīn rú liú shuǐ, yí qù bú fù huí

光阴如流水，一去不复回。

光陰如流水，一去不復回。

Time is like a river - it flows by and doesn't return.

guāng yīn sì jiàn, suì yuè rú suō

光阴似箭，岁月如梭。

光陰似箭，歲月如梭。

Time flies like an arrow.

guì rén duō wàng shì

贵人多忘事。

貴人多忘事。

Distinguished persons are apt to be forgetful.

gǔn shí bù shēng tāi, zhuǎn yè bú jù cái

滚石不生苔, 转业不聚财。

滾石不生苔, 轉業不聚財。

A rolling stone gathers no moss, and one who changes professions accumulates no wealth.

guó jiā xīng wáng, pǐ fū yǒu zé

国家兴亡, 匹夫有责。

國家興亡, 匹夫有責。

Every man has a share of responsibility for the fate of his country.

guó yǐ mín wéi běn, mín yǐ shí wéi tiān

国以民为本, 民以食为天。

國以民為本, 民以食為天。

The people are the foundation of the state, and food is vital to the people.

guó zhī běn zài jiā, jiā zhī běn zài shēn

国之本在家, 家之本在身。

國之本在家, 家之本在身。

The foundation of a nation is the family, and the foundation of a family is the individual.

guò ěr bù gǎi, shì wéi guò yi

过而不改, 是为过矣。

過而不改, 是為過矣。

It is a mistake to make a mistake but not correct it.

guò ěr néng gǎi, shàn mò dà yān

过而能改, 善莫大焉。

過而能改, 善莫大焉。

The ability to correct a mistake is a wonderful thing.

H

há mā yǒu shí yě huì bèi ní xiàn zhù
蛤蟆有时也会被泥陷住。
蛤蟆有時也會被泥陷住。
Even frogs sometimes get stuck in the mud.

hài rén zhī xīn bù kě yǒu, fáng rén zhī xīn bù kě wú
害人之心不可有, 防人之心不可无。
害人之心不可有, 防人之心不可無。
Have no intent to harm anyone, yet maintain a state of vigilance.

hán bù zé yī, jī bù zé shí
寒不择衣, 饥不择食
寒不擇衣, 飢不擇食
When cold, any clothes will do; when hungry, any food will do.
Beggars cannot be choosers.

háng háng chū zhuàng yuán
行行出状元。
行行出狀元。
Every field produces its own leading authority.

háng háng yǒu lì, háng háng yǒu bì

行行有利, 行行有弊。

行行有利, 行行有弊。

There are pros and cons to every line of work.

háo mén duō niè zǐ

豪门多孽子。

豪門多孽子。

Rich families have more unfilial sons.

hǎo chá bú pà xì pǐn, hǎo shì bú pà xì lùn

好茶不怕细品, 好事不怕细论。

好茶不怕細品, 好事不怕細論。

Good tea can pass a taste test, and good deeds can stand up to examination.

hǎo de kāi shǐ shì chéng gōng de yí bàn

好的开始是成功的一半。

好的開始是成功的一半。

Well begun is half done.

hǎo gǒu bù dǎng lù

好狗不挡路

好狗不擋路

A good dog does not get in the way.

hǎo gǒu bù yǎo jī, hǎo hàn bù dǎ qī

好狗不咬鸡, 好汉不打妻。

好狗不咬雞, 好漢不打妻。

A good dog won't attack the chickens, and a good man won't beat his wife.

hǎo hàn bù chī yǎn qián kuī

好汉不吃眼前亏。

好漢不吃眼前虧。

A wise man will not fight against impossible odds.

hǎo hàn píng zhì qiáng, hǎo mǎ píng dǎn zhuàng

好汉凭志强, 好马凭胆壮。

好漢憑志強, 好馬憑膽壯。

Great men rely on great ambition as good horses rely on courage.

hǎo hàn zuò shì hǎo hàn dāng

好汉做事好汉当。

好漢做事好漢當。

A great man takes responsibility for his actions.

hǎo huà sān biàn, lián gǒu yě xián

好话三遍, 连狗也嫌。

好話三遍, 連狗也嫌。

Even dogs tire of hearing the same praise again and again.

hǎo huò bú pà shì, pà shì méi hǎo huò

好货不怕试，怕试没好货。

好貨不怕試，怕試沒好貨。

High-quality products can stand up to a test; products that cannot stand up to a test are not of high quality.

hǎo huò bù pián yí, pián yí wú hǎo huò

好货不便宜，便宜无好货。

好貨不便宜，便宜無好貨。

High-quality merchandise is not cheap, and cheap things are not high-quality merchandise.

hǎo jì xìng bù rú làn bǐ tóu

好记性不如烂笔头。

好記性不如爛筆頭。

A good memory is not as good as an average pen.
Write it down, so you won't forget.

hǎo jiàng bù shuō dāng nián yǒng

好将不说当年勇。

好將不說當年勇。

The capable general does not refer to his past exploits.

hǎo jǐng bù cháng zài

好景不常在。

好景不常在。

Good times don't last long.

hǎo jù bù rú hǎo sàn

好聚不如好散。

好聚不如好散。

Better to depart on good terms than to arrive on good terms.

hǎo kàn de huā ér wèi bì xiāng

好看的花儿未必香。

好看的花兒未必香。

Pretty flowers are not necessarily fragrant.

hǎo lái bù rú hǎo qù

好来不如好去。

好來不如好去。

Better to depart on good terms than to arrive on good terms.

hǎo mǎ bù chī huí tóu cǎo

好马不吃回头草。

好馬不吃回頭草。

A good horse will not turn back for a mouthful of grass.
A person of accomplishment will keep moving forward.

hǎo mǎ bù tíng tí, hǎo niú bù tíng lí

好马不停蹄, 好牛不停犁。

好馬不停蹄, 好牛不停犁。

A good horse never stops moving and a good ox never stops
pulling.

hǎo rén bù cháng shòu, huài rén huó bǎi nián

好人不长寿，坏人活百年。

好人不長壽，壞人活百年。

The good die young while the bad live to one hundred.

hǎo rén shuō bú huài, hǎo jiǔ jiǎo bù suān

好人说不坏，好酒搅不酸。

好人說不壞，好酒攪不酸。

Gossip won't harm a good person as stirring won't spoil good wine.

hǎo shí mó dāo yě yào shuǐ

好石磨刀也要水。

好石磨刀也要水。

When sharpening a knife, even the finest stone needs water.

hǎo shì bú guò sān

好事不过三。

好事不過三。

Fortune knocks but thrice.

hǎo shì bù chū mén, huài shì chuán qiān lǐ

好事不出门，坏事传里。

好事不出門，壞事傳千里。

Good news travels slowly, while bad news travels quickly.

hǎo shì duō mó

好事多磨。

好事多磨。

The road to happiness is filled with setbacks.

hǎo shǒu nán xiù méi xiàn huā

好手难绣没线花。

好手難繡沒線花。

Even a skilled craftsman needs thread to embroider a flower.

hǎo shū bú yàn bǎi huí dú

好书不厌百回读。

好書不厭百回讀。

Good books retain their flavor after one hundred readings.

hǎo tiě bù dǎ dīng, hǎo nán bù dāng bīng

好铁不打钉, 好男不当兵。

好鐵不打釘, 好男不當兵。

Good iron is not used for nails, and good men are not used as soldiers.

hǎo xié bù cǎi chòu gǒu shǐ

好鞋不踩臭狗屎。

好鞋不踩臭狗屎。

Good shoes don't step in dog excrement.
Good people do not mingle with scoundrels.

hǎo zhú chū hǎo xǔn

好竹出好笋。

好竹出好筍。

Good bamboo produces good bamboo shoots.
Good children come from good parents.

hào dòu de gōng jī bù zhǎng máo

好斗的公鸡不长毛。

好鬥的公雞不長毛。

The cock that loves to fight grows no hair.

hào jiào de māo dǎo bú dào lǎo shǔ

好叫的猫逮不到老鼠。

好叫的貓逮不到老鼠。

Cats that love to purr don't catch mice.

hē shuǐ bú wàng jué jǐng rén

喝水不忘掘井人。

喝水不忘掘井人。

When drinking from a well, remember the one who dug it.
Be grateful for your blessings.

hé lǐ yān sǐ huì shuǐ rén

河里淹死会水人。

河裡淹死會水人。

Good swimmers drown in the river.
Capable people often fail due to carelessness.

hé qì shēng cái

和气生财。

和氣生財。

Amiability leads to wealth.

hé yǒu liǎng àn, shì yǒu liǎng miàn

河有两岸, 事有两面。

河有兩岸, 事有兩面。

Rivers have two banks, and every issue has two sides.

hóng yán duō bó mìng

红颜多薄命。

紅顏多薄命。

The fairest flowers soonest fade.

hòu shàng chuán zhě xiān xià àn

后上船者先下岸。

後上船者先下岸。

The last to embark is the first to debark.

hǔ dú bù shí zi

虎毒不食子。

虎毒不食子。

Even the vicious tiger will not eat its offspring.

hǔ fù wú quǎn zǐ

虎父无犬子。

虎父無犬子。

A tiger father will not produce a dog son.

huā měi měi yì shí, rén měi měi yí shì

花美美一时，人美美一世。

花美美一時，人美美一世。

A flower's beauty is fleeting, but a person's beauty lasts a lifetime.

huā yǒu chóng kāi rì, rén wú zài shào nián

花有重开日，人无再少年。

花有重開日，人無再少年。

Flowers may bloom again, but man never recaptures his youth.

huà bú yào shuō sǐ, lù bú yào zuǒ jué

话不要说死，路不要走绝。

話不要說死，路不要走絕。

Do not issue ultimatums and do not travel down the road of no return.

huà bù tóu jī bàn jù duō

话不投机半句多。

話不投機半句多。

When a conversation turns sour, to say one more word is a waste of breath.

huà duō bù tián, jiāo duō bù nián

话多不甜, 胶多不黏。

話多不甜, 膠多不黏。

Too many words are unpleasant, and too much glue is not sticky.

huà duō le shāng rén, shí duō le shāng shēn

话多了伤人, 食多了伤身。

話多了傷人, 食多了傷身。

Too much talk harms a person, and too much food harms the body.

huà hǔ huà pí nán huà gǔ, zhī rén zhī miàn bù zhī xīn

画虎画皮难画骨, 知人知面不知心。

畫虎畫皮難畫骨, 知人知面不知心。

In drawing a tiger, you draw the skin but not the bones; knowing a man, you know his face but not his heart.

huān chǎng nǚ ér zhēn wú qíng

欢场女儿真无情。

歡場女兒真無情。

Women who enjoy the nightlife have the coldest hearts.

huàn nàn jiàn zhēn qíng

患难见真情。

患難見真情。

Through calamities, one sees true friendship.
A friend in need is a friend indeed.

huáng hé yǒu dǐ, rén xīn wú dǐ

黄河有底, 人心无底。

黄河有底, 人心無底。

There is a bottom to the Huang River, but none to the human heart.

huáng tiān bú fù kǔ xīn rén

皇天不负苦心人。

皇天不負苦心人。

Heaven will reward the diligent.

huì dǎ huì suàn, liáng shí bú duàn

会打会算, 粮食不断。

會打會算, 糧食不斷。

He who plans accordingly will always have food.

huì jiào de gǒu, bú huì yǎo rén

会叫的狗, 不会咬人。

會叫的狗, 不會咬人。

A barking dog seldom bites.

huì shuō bù rú huì tīng

会说不如会听。

會說不如會聽。

It's better to know how to listen than how to talk.

huì xuǎn de xuǎn ér láng, bú huì xuǎn de xuǎn jiā dàng

会选的选儿郎, 不会选的选家当。

會選的選兒郎, 不會選的選家當。

Those who know how to choose will pick the son-in-law, and those who don't know how to choose will pick the property.

hūn lǐ pū zhāng, liǎng bài jù shāng

婚礼铺张, 两败俱伤。

婚禮鋪張, 兩敗俱傷。

An extravagant wedding hurts both sides of the family.

huó dào lǎo, xué dào lǎo

活到老, 学到老。

活到老, 學到老。

One is never too old to learn.

huǒ jí lào bù hǎo bǐng, huǒ měng shāo bù hǎo fàn

火急烙不好饼, 火猛烧不好饭。

火急烙不好餅, 火猛燒不好飯。

Too much heat cannot cook good food.
Haste makes waste.

huò fú wéi lín

祸福为邻。

禍福為鄰。

Fortune and misfortune are neighbors.

huò fú wú mén, wéi rén zì zhāo

祸福无门，唯人自招。

禍福無門，唯人自招。

There are no doors leading to fortune or misfortune - your actions will determine which one you choose.

huò nán rù shèn jiā zhī mén

祸难入慎家之门。

禍難入慎家之門。

It is hard for misfortune to enter the home of a cautious family.

huò wèn sān jiā bù chī kuī

货问三家不吃亏。

貨問三家不吃虧。

Shop around and you'll never be cheated.

huò xī fú suǒ yǐ, fú xī huò suǒ fú

祸兮福所倚，福兮祸所伏。

禍兮福所倚，福兮禍所伏。

Good fortune lies within bad, and bad fortune lurks within good.

J

jī dù nǎ zhī yā dù

鸡肚那知鸦肚。

雞肚那知鴉肚。

How can a chicken understand how a duck thinks?

jī è zhě sàng

积恶者丧。

積惡者喪。

Those who accumulate bad deeds will fall into decline.

jī féi bú xià dàn

鸡肥不下蛋。

雞肥不下蛋。

Plump hens lay no eggs.

jī shàn zhě chāng

积善者昌。

積善者昌。

Those who accumulate good deeds will prosper.

jī shàn zhī jiā, bì yǒu yú qìng

积善之家, 必有余庆。

積善之家, 必有餘慶。

Those who accumulate good deeds will have much to celebrate.

jī shǎo chéng duō

积少成多。

積少成多。

Small accumulations lead to great realizations.
Many a little makes a mickle.

jī sī chéng lǚ, jī cùn chéng chǐ

积丝成缕, 积寸成尺。

積絲成縷, 積寸成尺。

Many a little makes a mickle.

jī yǔ chén zhōu

积羽沉舟。

積羽沉舟。

Pile up enough feathers and one can sink a boat.

jí bìng zài zhì, màn bìng zài yǎng

急病在治, 慢病在养。

急病在治, 慢病在養。

An acute illness requires treatment while a chronic illness requires recuperation.

jí fēng zhī jìng cǎo

疾风知劲草。

疾風知勁草。

The force of the wind tests the strength of the grass.

jǐ suǒ bú yù, wù shī yú rén

己所不欲, 勿施于人。

己所不欲, 勿施於人。

Do not do unto others what you would not like others to do unto you.

jiā bù hé, wài rén qī

家不和, 外人欺。

家不和, 外人欺。

Disharmony within the home leads to outside attacks.

jiā chǒu bù kě wài yáng

家丑不可外扬。

家醜不可外揚。

Don't wash dirty laundry in public.

jiā hé wàn shì xīng

家和万事兴。

家和萬事興。

If the family lives in harmony, all affairs will prosper.

jiā jiā yǒu běn nán niàn de jīng

家家有本难念的经。

家家有本難唸的經。

Every household has it own tale of woe.

jiā lǐ yǒu ge jié yuē shǒu, yì nián chī chuān dōu bù chóu

家里有个节约手, 一年吃穿都不愁。

家裡有個節約手, 一年吃穿都不愁。

If there is a thrifty person in the family, you don't have to worry about not having enough to eat and wear.

jiā pín chū xiào zǐ, guó nàn xiǎn zhōng chén

家贫出孝子, 国难显忠臣。

家貧出孝子, 國難顯忠臣。

Poor families produce dutiful sons, and loyal officials stand out in times of national crisis.

jiā yǒu qiān jīn, bù jí rì jìn fēn wén

家有千金, 不及日进分文。

家有千金, 不及日進分文。

Better to have a modest but steady income than one thousand pieces of gold.

jiā yǒu xián qī, fū yǒu xián yì

家有贤妻, 夫有闲逸。

家有賢妻, 夫有閒逸。

Good wife, carefree husband.

jiā zhōng yǒu yì lǎo, hǎo sì yǒu yì bǎo

家中有一老, 好似有一宝。

家中有一老, 好似有一寶。

An elder in the home is like a treasure.

jià bù néng quàn yì biān, kàn rén bù néng kàn yí miàn

架不能劝一边, 看人不能看一面。

架不能勸一邊, 看人不能看一面。

You can't break up a fight by trying to pacify one party, and you can't judge a person by looking at only one facet of his character.

jià jī suí jī, jià gǒu suí gǒu

嫁鸡随鸡, 嫁狗随狗。

嫁雞隨雞, 嫁狗隨狗。

Marry a chicken and follow the chicken; marry a dog and follow the dog.

Be loyal to the man you marry, whether he be a fool or a crook.

jiān tīng zé míng, piān xìn zé àn

兼听则明, 偏信则暗。

兼聽則明, 偏信則暗。

Listen to both sides and be enlightened; listen to one side and be deceived.

jiǎn le zhī má, diū le xī guā

捡了芝麻, 丢了西瓜。

撿了芝麻, 丢了西瓜。

Pick up the sesame seeds but overlook the watermelons.

Penny wise and pound foolish.

jiàn guài bú guài, qí guài zì bài

见怪不怪, 其怪自败。

見怪不怪, 其怪自敗。

When a strange thing is not recognized as strange, its strangeness disappears.

jiàn quán de jīng shén yù yú jiàn quán de shēn tǐ

健全的精神寓于健全的身体。

健全的精神寓于健全的身體。

A sound mind in a healthy body.

jiàn yì sī qiān, yè nán chéng

见异思迁, 业难成。

見異思遷, 業難成。

You can't succeed if you keeping changing course.

jiāng shān yì gǎi, běn xìng nán yí

江山易改, 本性难移。

江山易改, 本性難移。

While rivers can be channeled and mountains moved, the hardest thing is to change the nature of man.
The leopard cannot change his spots.

jiāng shì lǎo de là

姜是老的辣。

薑是老的辣。

With age comes wisdom.

jiàng xiàng běn wú zhǒng, nán ér dāng zì qiáng

将相本无种, 男儿当自强。

將相本無種, 男兒當自強。

Masters are made, not born.

jiàng zài mǒu ěr bú zài yǒng, bīng zài jīng ěr bú zài duō

将在谋而不在勇, 兵在精而不在多。

將在謀而不在勇, 兵在精而不在多。

Generals are valued for their strategic abilities rather than their battlefield courage; soldiers are valued for their quality rather than their quantity.

jiāo ào shì shèng lì de dí rén

骄傲是胜利的敌人。

驕傲是勝利的敵人。

Arrogance is the enemy of victory.

jiāo qiǎn bù kě yán shēn

交浅不可言深。

交淺不可言深。

Don't have deep discussions with casual acquaintances.

jiāo rén jiāo xīn, jiāo huā jiāo gēn

交人交心, 浇花浇根。

交人交心, 澆花澆根。

Make friends from the heart and water flowers at the root.

jiāo yǒu fēn hòu bó, chuān yī kàn hán shǔ

交友分厚薄，穿衣看寒暑。

交友分厚薄，穿衣看寒暑。

Distinguish between close and distant friends as you distinguish between summer and winter clothes.

jiāo zǐ cóng xiǎo qǐ, zhì jiā qín jiǎn qǐ

教子从小起，治家勤俭起。

教子從小起，治家勤儉起。

The education of children begins when they are small and the management of a household begins with industry and frugality.

jiǎo tù yǒu sān kū

狡兔有三窟。

狡兔有三窟。

The clever hare has three burrows.

jié yuē hǎo bǐ yàn xián ní, liàng fèi hǎo bǐ hé jué tí

节约好比燕衔泥，浪费好比河决堤。

節約好比燕銜泥，浪費好比河決堤。

Thrift is like a swallow carrying a pinch of earth in its beak while extravagance is like a dam that has burst.

jié zú xiān dēng

捷足先登。

捷足先登。

The early bird catches the worm.

jiě líng hái xū xì líng rén

解铃还需系铃人。

解鈴還需繫鈴人。

The one who creates the mess should untangle it.

jiè lái de yī shang bù hé tǐ

借来的衣裳不合体。

借來的衣裳不合體。

Borrowed clothes don't fit well.

jīn píng huǒ liàn, rén píng xīn jiāo

金凭火炼, 人凭心交。

金憑火煉, 人憑心交。

Gold is forged in fire as friendship is formed through open hearts.

jīn rì qiě chī jīn rì fàn, míng tiān yǒu shì míng tiān bàn

今日且吃今日饭, 明天有事明天办。

今日且吃今日飯, 明天有事明天辦。

Eat today's food today and take care of tomorrow's work tomorrow.

jīn rì shì, jīn rì bì

今日事, 今日毕。

今日事, 今日畢。

Finish today's work today.

jǐn kāi kǒu, màn xǔ nuò

谨开口, 慢许诺。

謹開口, 慢許諾。

Be prudent in speech and in promises.

jǐn zhēng yǎn, màn zhāng kǒu

紧睁眼, 慢张口。

緊睜眼, 慢張口。

Keep your eyes wide open, but open your mouth slowly.

jìn lín bù kě duàn, yuǎn yǒu bù kě shū

近邻不可断, 远友不可疏。

近鄰不可斷, 遠友不可疏。

Talk to your neighbors and keep in contact with distant friends.

jìn xìn shū, bù rú bù dú shū

尽信书, 不如不读书。

盡信書, 不如不讀書。

If you believe everything you read, then you had better not read.

jìn zhū zhě chì, jìn mò zhě hēi

近朱者赤, 近墨者黑。

近朱者赤, 近墨者黑。

He who handles vermillion will be reddened, and he who touches ink will be blackened.

He who keeps company with the wolf will learn to howl.

jīng chéng suǒ zhì, jīn shí wéi kāi

精诚所至, 金石为开。

精誠所至, 金石為開。

No difficulty is insurmountable if one is determined.

jīng gōng jiàng bù rú qiǎo zhǔ rén

精工匠不如巧主人。

精工匠不如巧主人。

Better a clever master than a skilled craftsman.

jǐng shuǐ bú fàn hé shuǐ

井水不犯河水。

井水不犯河水。

Well water does not encroach upon river water.
I'll mind my business and you mind yours.

jiǔ bìng chéng liáng yī

久病成良医。

久病成良醫。

Prolonged illness makes a doctor of a patient.

jiǔ bìng wú xiào zǐ

久病无孝子。

久病無孝子。

There are no filial children at the bedside of chronically ill parents.

jiǔ céng zhī tái, qǐ yú liě tǔ

九层之台, 起于垒土。

九層之臺, 起于壘土。

A nine-story terrace rises through a gradual accumulation of bricks and mud.

jiǔ dǔ wú shèng jiā

久赌无胜家。

久賭無勝家。

There are no winners among habitual gamblers.

jiǔ hòu tǔ zhēn yán

酒后吐真言。

酒後吐真言。

In wine there is truth.

jiǔ néng chéng shì, yě néng bài shì

酒能成事, 也能败事。

酒能成事, 也能敗事。

Wine can make you succeed or make you fail.

jiǔ ruò péng yǒu hǎo zhǎo, huàn nàn zhī jiāo nán féng

酒肉朋友好找, 患难之交难逢。

酒肉朋友好找, 患難之交難逢。

It's easy to find friends for a good time, but it's hard to find friends in bad times.

jiǔ ruò péng yǒu, méi qián fēn shǒu

酒肉朋友，没钱分手。

酒肉朋友，沒錢分手。

Friends made during merrymaking part ways when the money runs out.

jiǔ zhù pō, bù xián dǒu

久住坡，不嫌陡。

久住坡，不嫌陡。

Those who live long on the hillside do not mind the slope.

jiù de bú qù, xīn de bù lái

旧的不去，新的不来。

舊的不去，新的不來。

If the old is not gone, the new will not come.

jù shā chéng tǎ

聚沙成塔。

聚沙成塔。

Many grains of sand piled up will make a pagoda.
Many a little makes a mickle.

juān juān zhī dī, huì chéng jiāng hé

涓涓之滴，汇成江河。

涓涓之滴，匯成江河。

Many little drops forge a river.

jūn zǐ bào chóu, shí nián bù wǎn
君子报仇，十年不晚。
君子報仇，十年不晚。
Ten years is not too long for a gentleman to wait for revenge.

jūn zǐ bù shī chì zǐ zhī xīn
君子不失赤子之心。
君子不失赤子之心。
A gentleman is one who has not lost the heart of a child.

jūn zǐ mǒu dào bù mǒu shí
君子谋道不谋食。
君子謀道不謀食。
Righteous men seek truth, not sustenance.

jūn zǐ yǐ gōng bào dé, xiǎo rén jì chóu wàng ēn
君子以功报德，小人记仇忘恩。
君子以功報德，小人記仇忘恩。
Gentlemen repay kindness with good deeds while scoundrels hold onto grudges and forget about favors received.

jūn zǐ yǒu chéng rén zhī měi
君子有成人之美。
君子有成人之美。
A gentleman has the virtue of helping others achieve their goals.

jūn zǐ zhī jiāo dàn rú shuǐ

君子之交淡如水。

君子之交淡如水。

Friendship between gentlemen appears indifferent but is pure like water.

K

kāi gōng méi yǒu huí tóu jiàn
开弓没有回头箭。
開弓沒有回頭箭。
The arrow once released cannot be retrieved.

kāi juàn yǒu yì
开卷有益。
開卷有益。
Read and reap the rewards.

kàn huā róng yì, xiù huā nán
看花容易, 绣花难。
看花容易, 繡花難。
It is easy to look at a flower, but difficult to embroider one.

kàn rén tiāo dàn bù chī lì
看人挑担不吃力。
看人挑擔不吃力。
The load carried by another does not seem heavy.

kào rén dóu shì jiǎ, dié dǎo zì jǐ pá

靠人都是假, 跌倒自己爬。

靠人都是假, 跌倒自己爬。

You can't rely on others, and you get up on your own when you fall down.

kào shān chī shān, kào shuǐ chī shuǐ

靠山吃山, 靠水吃水。

靠山吃山, 靠水吃水。

Those living on the mountain live off of the mountain, and those living near water live off of the water.

kōng tǒng xiǎng dīng dāng

空桶响叮当。

空桶響叮噹。

Empty vessels make the most noise.

kǒu shuō wú píng, shì shí wéi zhèng

口说无凭, 事实为证。

口說無憑, 事實為證。

Talk is not proof, but facts are evidence.
The proof of the pudding is in the eating.

kǔ hǎi wú biān, huí tóu shì àn

苦海无边, 回头是岸。

苦海無邊, 回頭是岸。

The sea of bitterness knows no bounds, but repent and the shore is near.

kuài rén yì yán, kuài mǎ yì biān

快人一言, 快马一鞭。

快人一言, 快馬一鞭。

A few words to the wise will suffice.

kuài zhī wú hǎo shā, kuài jià wú hǎo jiā

快织无好纱, 快嫁无好家。

快織無好紗, 快嫁無好家。

Weave fast and the yarn is no good; marry in haste and the family is no good.

kuī rén shì huò

亏人是祸。

虧人是禍。

Mistreating people is a form of misfortune.

kùn lóng yě yǒu shàng tiān shí

困龙也有上天时。

困龍也有上天時。

Even troubled dragons will have a chance to fly.
Every dog has its day.

L

lái ěr bù wǎng, fēi lǐ yě
来而不往, 非礼也。
來而不往, 非禮也。
It's impolite not to give after receiving.

lǎn hé shàng zuò bù chū hǎo zhā lái
懒和尚做不出好斋来。
懶和尚做不出好齋來。
Lazy monks don't prepare tasty meals.

lǎn māo dǎi bú dào sǐ lǎo shǔ
懒猫逮不到死老鼠。
懶貓逮不到死老鼠。
A lazy cat won't even catch a dead mouse.

làng zǐ huí tóu jīn bú huàn
浪子回头金不换。
浪子回頭金不換。
The prodigal son who reforms is more precious than gold.

láo xīn zhě zhì rén, láo lì zhě zhì yú rén

劳心者治人，劳力者治于人。

勞心者治人，勞力者治於人。

Those who work with their brains rule while those who work
with their brawn are ruled.

lǎo gǒu xué bù lái xīn huā yàng

老狗学不来新花样。

老狗學不來新花樣。

You can't teach an old dog new tricks.

lǎo hǔ chī rén yì dǒu, rén yào chī rén nán fáng

老虎吃人易躲，人要吃人难防。

老虎吃人易躲，人要吃人難防。

It is easy to dodge a tiger, but it is hard to guard against
people.

lǎo hǔ huā zài bèi, rén xīn huā zài nèi

老虎花在背，人心花在内。

老虎花在背，人心花在內。

A tiger's pattern is on his back and a person's machinations
are in his heart.

lǎo hǔ yě yǒu dǎ kùn shí

老虎也有打盹时。

老虎也有打盹時。

Even the tiger dozes off .
No one is perfect.

lǎo niú hǎo shǐ

老牛好使。

老牛好使。

Old cows are easier to manage.

lǎo rén xiū qǔ shào nián qī

老人休娶少年妻。

老人休娶少年妻。

Old men shouldn't marry young wives.

lǎo wáng mài guā, zì mài zì kuā

老王卖瓜, 自卖自夸。

老王賣瓜, 自賣自誇。

The melon seller boasts about the melons he is selling.

Every cook commends his own sauce.

léi shēng dà, yǔ diǎn xiǎo

雷声大, 雨点小。

雷聲大, 雨點小。

Thunder roars loudly, but little rain falls.

lěng tiě nán dǎ, lǎo zhú nán wān

冷铁难打, 老竹难弯。

冷鐵難打, 老竹難彎。

Cold iron is hard to forge and old bamboo is hard to bend.

lěng zhōu lěng fàn hǎo chī, lěng yán lěng yǔ nán shòu

冷粥冷饭好吃, 冷言冷语难受。

冷粥冷飯好吃, 冷言冷語難受。

A cold meal is acceptable, but sarcastic comments are hard to take.

lǐ bú biàn bù míng, huà bù shuō bù qīng

理不辩不明, 话不讲不清。

理不辯不明, 話不講不清。

Truth is established through debate as words become clear when spoken.

lǐ duō bì zhà

礼多必诈。

禮多必詐。

Excessive politeness conceals deceit.

lǐ zhèng bú qù fǎ

理正不怯法。

理正不怯法。

Those who are upright fear not the law.

lǐ zhì hǎo rén, fǎ zhì huài rén

理治好人, 法制坏人。

理治好人, 法制壞人。

Good people are ruled by the rules of propriety while bad people are ruled by laws.

lì rùn dà, fēng xiǎn dà

利润大, 风险大。

利潤大, 風險大。

If the profits are great, the risks are great.

liàn tiě xū yào liè huǒ, jiāo yǒu xū yào chéng xīn

炼铁需要烈火, 交友需要诚心。

煉鐵需要烈火, 交友需要誠心。

Forging iron requires strong fire, and making friends
requires sincerity.

liáng jiàng wú qì cái

良匠无弃材

良匠無棄材

The skilled craftsman will discard nothing.

liáng yán rù ěr sān dōng nuǎn, è yán shāng rén liù yuè hán

良言入耳三冬暖, 恶言伤人六月寒。

良言入耳三冬暖, 惡言傷人六月寒。

Good words warm a person up for three winters, while bad
words chill the heart even in the heat of summer.

liáng yào kǔ kǒu, zhōng yán nì ěr

良药苦口, 忠言逆耳。

良藥苦口, 忠言逆耳。

Just as bitter medicine cures sickness, unpalatable advice
benefits conduct.

liǎng hǔ xiāng zhēng, bì yǒu yì shāng

两虎相争，必有一伤。

兩虎相爭，必有一傷。

When two tigers battle, one will get hurt.
Diamond cuts diamond.

liǎng rén yǎng mǎ shòu, liǎng rén yǎng chuán lòu

两人养马瘦，两人养船漏。

兩人養馬瘦，兩人養船漏。

A horse raised by two people will be skinny, and the boat
tended by two people will leak.

liè huǒ jiàn chún jīn

烈火见纯金。

烈火見純金。

Pure gold fears not fire.

lín jiā shī huǒ, bú jiù zì wéi

邻家失火，不救自危。

鄰家失火，不救自危。

When the neighbor's house is on fire, you put yourself in
danger if you don't help extinguish it.

lín shè hǎo, wú jià bǎo

邻舍好，无价宝。

鄰舍好，無價寶。

A good neighborhood is a priceless treasure.

lín zhèn mó dāo wǎn

临阵磨刀晚。

臨陣磨刀晚。

It is too late to sharpen your sword on the brink of battle.

liú shuǐ bú chòu, chòu shuǐ bù liú

流水不臭，臭水不流。

流水不臭，臭水不流。

Flowing water does not stink and stinky water does not flow.

liú shuǐ bù fǔ, hù shū bù dǔ

流水不腐，户枢不蠹。

流水不腐，戶樞不蠹。

Flowing water does not stink and a door hinge does not become worm eaten.

lóng dōng zhī hòu, bì yǒu yáng chūn

隆冬之后，必有阳春。

隆冬之後，必有陽春。

After a heavy winter comes a sunny spring.

lóng shēng lóng, fèng shēng fèng, hào zi shēng lái huì dǎ dòng

龙生龙，凤生凤，耗子生来会打洞。

龍生龍，鳳生鳳，耗子生來會打洞。

A dragon will produce a dragon, a phoenix will produce a phoenix, and the baby mouse knows how to dig a hole.

Like father like son.

lóng yóu qiǎn shuǐ zāo xiā xì, hǔ luò píng yáng bèi quǎn qī

龙游浅水遭虾戏, 虎落平阳被犬欺。

龍游淺水遭蝦戲, 虎落平陽被犬欺。

When the dragon dives into shallow water, it will be jeered at by the shrimp; when the tiger descends to the valley, it will be picked on by the dog.

liú dé qīng shān zài, bú pà méi chái shāo

留得青山在, 不怕没柴烧。

留得青山在, 不怕沒柴燒。

As long as there are forests, one need not worry about firewood.

lù shàng shuō huà, cǎo lǐ yǒu rén

路上说话, 草里有人。

路上說話, 草裡有人。

Be careful about talking on the road because there might be people in the bushes.

Walls have ears.

lù shì zǒu shóu de, shì shì zuò shùn de

路是走熟的, 事是做顺的。

路是走熟的, 事是做順的。

Walk a road and it becomes familiar; do a job and it becomes easy.

lù yáo zhī mǎ lì, rì jiǔ jiàn rén xīn

路遥知马力, 日久见人心。

路遙知馬力, 日久見人心。

As a long road tests a horse's strength, a man's character will be revealed over time.

M

má què suī xiǎo, wǔ zàng jù quán

麻雀虽小，五脏俱全。

麻雀雖小，五臟俱全。

A sparrow may be small, but it has everything it needs.

mǎ hǎo bú zài chǎo, rén měi bú zài mào

马好不在吵，人美不在貌。

馬好不在吵，人美不在貌。

The worth of a horse is not judged by the noise it makes, and a person's beauty is not judged by external appearances.

mǎ kàn yá bǎn, rén kàn yán xíng

马看牙板，人看言行。

馬看牙板，人看言行。

Horses are judged by their teeth as people are judged by their conduct.

mǎ kào ān zhuāng, rén kào yī zhuāng

马靠鞍装，人靠衣装。

馬靠鞍裝，人靠衣裝。

Horses rely on saddles to dress them up as men rely on clothes to dress them up.

Fine feathers make fine birds.

mǎ lǎo shì lù tú, rén lǎo tōng shì gù

马老识路途, 人老通世故。

馬老識路途, 人老通世故。

An old horse knows the road and an old person knows the
ways of the world.

mǎ yǐ bān jiā, dà yù jiāng xià

蚂蚁搬家, 大雨将下。

螞蟻搬家, 大雨將下。

When ants move to a new home, it portends a heavy rain.

mǎi guō yào qiāo dǎ, qǔ jià yào xì chá

买锅要敲打, 娶嫁要细查。

買鍋要敲打, 娶嫁要細查。

When buying a pot, bang it first; when marrying, make
thorough inquiries first.

mǎi jìn tiān xià wù, nán mǎi zǐ sūn xián

买尽天下物, 难买子孙贤。

買盡天下物, 難買子孫賢。

You can buy anything for a price except virtue for your
offspring.

mǎi le pián yí chái shāo làn jiá dǐ guō

买了便宜柴, 烧烂夹底锅。

買了便宜柴, 燒爛夾底鍋。

Buy cheap wood, and it will burn your pot.

măi wū kàn liáng, qǔ qī kàn niáng

买屋看梁, 娶妻看娘。

買屋看樑, 娶妻看娘。

When buying a house, check the beams; when choosing a wife, check her mother.

mán tiān mán dì, mán bú guò lín jū

瞒天瞒地, 瞒不过邻居。

瞞天瞞地, 瞞不過鄰居。

You may deceive heaven and earth, but you can't deceive your neighbors.

măn píng bù xiǎng, bàn píng huǎng dàng

满瓶不响, 半瓶晃荡。

滿瓶不響, 半瓶晃盪。

A full bottle makes no sound, while a half-full bottle sloshes around.

măn zhāo sǔn, qiān shòu yì

满招损, 谦受益。

滿招損, 謙受益。

One loses by pride and gains by modesty.

màn bù dié bù dǎo, xiǎo xīn cuò bù liǎo

慢步跌不倒, 小心错不了。

慢步跌不倒, 小心錯不了。

Walk slowly and you won't fall down; act carefully and you won't make mistakes.

màn gōng chū xì huó

慢工出细活。

慢工出細活。

Steady application makes a superior product.

māo fā wēi yě chéng bù liǎo lǎo hǔ

猫发威也成不了老虎。

貓發威也成不了老虎。

The cat may shriek, but it will never become a tiger.

méi yǒu wú tóng shù, nǎ zhāo fèng huáng lái

没有梧桐树，哪招凤凰来。

沒有梧桐樹，哪招鳳凰來。

You can't attract a phoenix without a parasol tree.
You can't catch a fish without a worm.

měi féng jiē jié bèi sī qīn

每逢佳节倍思亲。

每逢佳節倍思親。

On festive occasions more than ever we think of our loved
ones far away.

měi mào shì quán néng, jīn qián shì wàn néng

美貌是全能，金钱是万能。

美貌是全能，金錢是萬能。

Beauty is potent but money is omnipotent.

měi míng nán dé ěr yì shī

美名难得而易失。

美名難得而易失。

A good reputation is hard to earn but easy to lose.

měi sè wú měi dé, hǎo bǐ huā wú xiāng

美色无美德, 好比花无香。

美色無美德, 好比花無香。

Beauty without virtue is like a flower with no fragrance.

mín yǐ shí wéi tiān

民以食为天。

民以食為天。

To the common folk, food is heaven.

mín yì bù kě wǔ

民意不可侮。

民意不可侮。

Public opinion cannot be coerced.

míng lì èr zì shì fēi duō

名利二字是非多。

名利二字是非多。

Fame and fortune lead to much trouble.

míng qiāng yì duǒ, àn jiàn nán fáng

明枪易躲，暗箭难防。

明槍易躲，暗箭難防。

It is easy to dodge a spear out in the open, but it's hard to guard against an arrow shot from a hiding place.

míng rén bú zuò àn shì

明人不做暗事。

明人不做暗事。

The honest person doesn't do shady things.

míng zhào àn shì, lǐ fú rén xīn

明照暗事，理服人心。

明照暗事，理服人心。

As light brightens a dark room, truth wins hearts and minds.

mǒu guān rú shǔ, dé guān rú hǔ

谋官如鼠，得官如虎

謀官如鼠，得官如虎

Act like a mouse when seeking an official post, and act like a tiger after acquiring the post.

mǒu shì zài rén, chéng shì zài tiān

谋事在人，成事在天。

謀事在人，成事在天。

Man proposes, God disposes.

N

nán pà rù cuò háng, nǚ pà jià cuò láng

男怕入错行，女怕嫁错郎。

男怕入錯行，女怕嫁錯郎。

Men should choose the right profession, and women should marry the right husband.

nán zǐ hàn dà zhàng fū, bù wéi wǔ dǒu mǐ zhé yāo

男子汉大丈夫，不为五斗米折腰。

男子漢大丈夫，不為五斗米折腰。

The true man will not compromise his principles for a meager reward.

néng zhě duō láo

能者多劳。

能者多勞。

The capable are given more work.

néng yán bú shì zhēn jūn zǐ, shàn chǔ cái shì dà zhàng fū

能言不是真君子，善处才是大丈夫。

能言不是真君子，善處才是大丈夫。

A true gentleman is not revealed by his eloquence, but by his good conduct.

nǐ jìng rén yí cùn, rén jìng nǐ yí zhàng

你敬人一寸, 人敬你一丈。

你敬人一寸, 人敬你一丈。

If you extend an inch of respect, you will receive a foot of respect in return.

nǐ kàn wǒ jiā hǎo, wǒ kàn nǐ jiā hǎo

你看我家好, 我看你家好。

你看我家好, 我看你家好。

The grass is greener on the other side of the fence.

nǐ qiáng kùn nán ruò, nǐ ruò kùn nán qiáng

你强困难弱, 你弱困难强。

你強困難弱, 你弱困難強。

If your mind is strong, all difficult things will become easy; if your mind is weak, all easy things will become difficult.

nǐ yǎng wǒ xiǎo, wǒ yǎng nǐ lǎo

你养我小, 我养你老。

你養我小, 我養你老。

You take care of me when I'm young, and I will take care of you when you're old.

nì fēng diǎn huǒ zì shāo shēn

逆风点火自烧身。

逆風點火自燒身。

Light a fire in the face of the wind and you will burn yourself.

niǎo guì yǒu yì, rén guì yǒu zhì

鸟贵有翼, 人贵有志。

鳥貴有翼, 人貴有志。

Wings are essential to a bird, and ambition is essential to a man.

niǎo zhī jiāng sǐ, qí míng yě āi;
rén zhī jiāng sǐ, qí yán yě shàn

鸟之将死, 其鸣也哀; 人之将死, 其言也善。

鳥之將死, 其鳴也哀; 人之將死, 其言也善。

When a bird is about to die, it cries plaintively; when a man is about to die, he speaks benevolently.

níng chī hǎo lí yí ge, bù chī làn lí yì kuāng

宁吃好梨一个, 不吃烂梨一筐。

寧吃好梨一個, 不吃爛梨一筐。

Better to eat one good pear than a whole basket of rotten ones.

níng fàn tiān gōng nù, mò fàn zhòng rén nǎo

宁犯天公怒, 莫犯众人恼。

寧犯天公怒, 莫犯眾人惱。

Better to arouse the anger of heaven than to arouse the anger of the masses.

níng hē péng yǒu de dàn chá, bù hē dí rén de mì jiǔ

宁喝朋友的淡茶, 不喝敌人的蜜酒。

寧喝朋友的淡茶, 不喝敵人的蜜酒。

Better to drink the weak tea of a friend than the sweet wine of an enemy.

níng kě chī cuò fàn, bù kě shuō cuò huà

宁可吃错饭, 不可说错话。

寧可吃錯飯, 不可說錯話。

Better to eat the wrong food than say the wrong words.

níng kě jié shēn ěr sǐ, bú yuàn wū shēn ěr shēng

宁可洁身而死, 不愿污身而生。

寧可潔身而死, 不願污身而生。

Better to be pure and die than to be sullied and live.
Death before dishonor.

níng kě wú qián, bù kě wú chǐ

宁可无钱, 不可无耻。

寧可無錢, 不可無恥。

Better to be poor than to be shameless.

níng kě shēn lěng, bù kě xīn lěng

宁可身冷, 不可心冷。

寧可身冷, 不可心冷。

Better a cold body than a cold heart.

níng kě yǎng yú bèn de hái zi, bù yǎng shuō huǎng de hái zi

宁可养愚笨的孩子, 不要养说谎的孩子。

寧可養愚笨的孩子, 不要養說謊的孩子。

Better to raise a child who isn't smart than a child who lies.

níng shě yí kuài jīn, bù shě yì xún chūn

宁舍一块金，不舍一旬春。

寧捨一塊金，不捨一旬春。

Better to give away a piece of gold than to give away a chunk of time.

níng wéi wū shàng niǎo, bú zuò fáng lǐ qiè

宁为屋上鸟，不做房里妾。

寧為屋上鳥，不做房裡妾。

Better to be a free bird on the roof than a wealthy concubine in the house.

níng wéi yù suì, bù wéi wǎ quán

宁为玉碎，不为瓦全。

寧為玉碎，不為瓦全。

Better to be a broken piece of jade than an intact roofing tile.
Better to die in glory than survive with dishonor.

níng zǒu shí bù yuǎn, bù zǒu yí bù xiǎn

宁走十步远，不走一步险。

寧走十步遠，不走一步險。

Better to take ten safe steps than a single dangerous one.
Better safe than sorry.

níng zuò jī tóu, bú zuò niú hòu

宁做鸡头，不做牛后。

寧做雞頭，不做牛後。

Better to be the head of a chicken than the tail of a cow.

nǚ dà shí bā biàn

女大十八变。

女大十八變。

When girls grow up, they undergo many changes.

nǚ dà shí bā yì duǒ huā

女大十八一朵花。

女大十八一朵花。

A girl at eighteen is like a flower.

nǚ rén xīn, hǎi dǐ zhēn

女人心，海底针

女人心，海底針

A woman's heart is as hard to fathom as fishing out a needle from the bottom of the ocean.

P

pá de gāo, dié de zhòng

爬得高, 跌得重。

爬得高, 跌得重。

The higher you climb, the harder you fall.

pà shuǐ dāng bù liǎo yú fū

怕水当不了渔夫。

怕水當不了漁夫。

Those afraid of the water can never become fishermen.

pà wèn lù, yào mí lù

怕问路, 要迷路。

怕問路, 要迷路。

Those who are afraid to ask directions will get lost.

pí zhī bù cún, máo jiāng yān fù

皮之不存, 毛将焉附。

皮之不存, 毛將焉附。

When the skin is gone, to what can the hair adhere?
Everything needs a foundation.

pín jiàn fū qī bǎi shì āi

贫贱夫妻百事哀。

貧賤夫妻百事哀。

For the poor couple, life is filled with sorrow.

pín zhě yīn shū ěr fù, fù zhě yīn shū ěr guì

贫者因书而富, 富者因书而贵。

貧者因書而富, 富者因書而貴。

The poor are enriched by books while the rich are
distinguished by books.

pó yǒu dé, xí fù xián

婆有德, 媳妇贤。

婆有德, 媳婦賢。

A virtuous mother-in-law will nurture a virtuous
daughter-in-law.

Q

qī ruǎn bì pà yìng

欺软必怕硬。

欺軟必怕硬。

Those who bully the weak are cowards before the strong.

qī shí èr biàn, běn xiàng nán biàn

七十二变, 本相难变。

七十二變, 本相難變。

Even with seventy-two transformations, it is still difficult to change one's true color.

qī shǒu bā jiǎo bì bài shì

七手八脚必败事。

七手八腳必敗事。

Too many cooks spoil the soup.

qǐ gài wú zhǒng, lǎn hàn zì chéng

乞丐无种, 懒汉自成。

乞丐無種, 懶漢自成。

One becomes a lazy beggar through no fault but his own.

qì dà shāng shén, shí dà shāng shēn

气大伤神，食大伤身。

氣大傷神，食大傷身。

Ecccessive anger harms the spirit, and excessive food harms the body.

qì kě gǔ ěr bù kě xiè

气可鼓而不可泄。

氣可鼓而不可泄。

Morale should be boosted, not dampened.

qì qiáng xiān dǎ jī, chī dàn xiān yǎng jī

砌墙先打基，吃蛋先养鸡。

砌牆先打基，吃蛋先養雞。

You must lay a foundation before you can build a wall, and you must raise a chicken before you can gather eggs.
Sow and you shall reap.

qì xiǎo yì yíng

器小易盈。

器小易盈。

Small vessels are quickly filled.

qiān jīn nán mǎi xīn tóu yuàn

千金难买心头愿。

千金難買心頭願。

One thousand pieces of gold can't buy what you long for in your heart.

qiān lǐ zhī dī, kuì yú yǐ xuè

千里之堤, 溃于蚁穴。

千里之堤, 潰于蟻穴。

A single ant hole may lead to the collapse of an enormous dike.

qiān lǐ zhī xíng, shǐ yú zú xià

千里之行, 始于足下。

千里之行, 始於足下。

A journey of one thousand miles begins with a single step.

qiān qiū dà yè, fēi yí rì zhī gōng

千秋大业, 非一日之功。

千秋大業, 非一日之功。

An enormous undertaking can't be accomplished in one day.

qiān xū bù rú yì shí

千虚不如一实。

千虚不如一實。

One thousand falsehoods are not as good as one truth.

qiān xū shì chéng gōng de péng yǒu

谦虚是成功的朋友。

謙虛是成功的朋友。

Modesty is the companion of success.

qián cái shēn wài wù

钱财身外物。

錢財身外物。

Money is not inherent to man.

qián cái yuè huā yuè shǎo, zhī shì yuè xué yuè duō

钱财越花越少，知识越学越多。

錢財越花越少，知識越學越多。

The more you spend, the less you have; the more you study, the more you know.

qián chē zhī fù, hòu chē zhī jiàn

前车之覆，后车之鉴。

前車之覆，後車之鑒。

The overturned cart up ahead serves as a warning to the carts behind.

Take heed of another man's mistake.

qián dào gōng shì bàn, huǒ dào zhū tóu làn

钱到公事办，火到猪头烂。

錢到公事辦，火到豬頭爛。

Money greases the wheels of business as fire roasts a succulent pig.

qián dào guāng gùn shǒu, yí qù bù huí tóu

钱到光棍手，一去不回头。

錢到光棍手，一去不回頭。

Money, in the hands of a bachelor, is as good as gone.

qián néng tōng shén

钱能通神。

錢能通神。

Money allows you to speak to the gods.

qián rén zhòng shù, hòu rén chéng liáng

前人种树, 后人乘凉。

前人種樹, 後人乘涼。

Each generation will reap what the former generation has sown.

qián shì bú wàng, hòu shì zhī shī

前事不忘, 后事之师。

前事不忘, 後事之師。

The past remembered is a good guide for the future.

qiàn zhài de duō jiàn wàng, tǎo zhài de jì xìng qiáng

欠债的多健忘, 讨债的记性强。

欠債的多健忘, 討債的記性強。

Debtors have short memories while creditors have long memories.

qiáng dǎo zhòng rén tuī

墙倒众人推。

牆倒眾人推。

When a wall starts to collapse, everyone will give it a push.

qiáng jì bù rú shàn wù

强记不如善悟。

強記不如善悟。

Forced memorization is not as good as natural realization.

qiáng jiàng shǒu xià wú ruò bīng

强将手下无弱兵。

強將手下無弱兵。

The skilled commander will lead an army of skilled soldiers.

qiáng yǒu fèng bì yǒu ěr

墙有缝壁有耳。

牆有縫壁有耳。

Walls have cracks; walls have ears.

qiáng zhōng zì yǒu qiáng zhōng shǒu

强中自有强中手。

強中自有強中手。

However strong you are, there is always someone stronger.

qiǎo fù nán wéi wú mǐ zhī chuī

巧妇难为无米之炊。

巧婦難為無米之炊。

Even the cleverest housewife cannot cook a meal without rice.
You cannot make something out of nothing.

qiǎo shǒu nán shǐ liǎng gēn zhēn

巧手难使两根针。

巧手難使兩根針。

Even a skilled hand cannot sew with two needles at the same time.

qiǎo yán lìng sè, xiǎn yú rén

巧言令色, 鲜于仁。

巧言令色, 鲜于仁。

Full of courtesy, full of craft.

qiǎo zhà bù rú jué chéng

巧诈不如拙诚。

巧詐不如拙誠。

Unintelligent sincerity is better than clever deception.

qiǎo zhě duō láo, zhuó zhě xián

巧者多劳, 拙者闲。

巧者多勞, 拙者閒。

The clever are entrusted with many tasks while the dull remain idle.

qīn suī qīn, cái bó fēn

亲虽亲, 财帛分。

親雖親, 財帛分。

Keep your money separate even from family members.

qīn xiōng dì, míng suàn zhàng

亲兄弟，明算帐。

親兄弟，明算帳。

Even brothers must settle accounts.

qín kuài rén yòng shǒu, lǎn duò rén yòng kǒu

勤快人用手，懒惰人用口。

勤快人用手，懶惰人用口。

Diligent persons use their hands while lazy ones use their mouths.

qín láo yì shòu, ān yì wáng shēn

勤劳益寿，安逸亡身。

勤勞益壽，安逸亡身。

Industry leads to longevity while leisure leads to doom.

qín lóng yào xià hǎi, dǎ hǔ yào shàng shān

擒龙要下海，打虎要上山。

擒龍要下海，打虎要上山。

You must go to sea to catch a dragon, and you must climb a mountain to catch a tiger.

qín niáng dài chū lǎn ér zi

勤娘带出懒儿子。

勤娘帶出懶兒子。

The mother who provides everything will raise a lazy son.

qín shì yáo qián shù, jiǎn shì jù bǎo pén

勤是摇钱树，俭是聚宝盆。

勤是搖錢樹，儉是聚寶盆。

Diligence is the tool that brings one riches and frugality is
the measure that helps keep them.

qín wéi wú jià bǎo, shèn shì hù shēn fú

勤为无价宝，慎是护身符。

勤為無價寶，慎是護身符。

Diligence is a priceless treasure, and caution is a talisman for
survival.

qín yǐ bǔ zhuó

勤以补拙。

勤以補拙。

Diligence will compensate for lack of natural skills.

qín yǐ zhì fù

勤以致富。

勤以致富。

Diligence leads to riches.

qín yǒu gōng, xī wú yì

勤有功，嬉无益。

勤有功，嬉無益。

Achievement comes from diligence, and nothing is gained by
fooling around.

qīng chái nán shāo, jiāo zǐ nán jiāo

青柴难烧，娇子难教。

青柴難燒，嬌子難教。

Green wood is hard to burn, and a pampered child is hard to teach.

qīng guān nán duàn jiā wù shì

清官难断家务事。

清官難斷家務事。

Even the fairest judge cannot settle a domestic dispute.

qīng jiǔ hóng rén miàn, cái bó dòng rén xīn

青酒红人面，财帛动人心。

青酒紅人面，財帛動人心。

Strong wine reddens the face, and wealth arouses the emotions.

qīng wā jiào, dà yǔ dào

青蛙叫，大雨到。

青蛙叫，大雨到。

When the frogs croak, a strong rain is on its way.

qíng hǎi wú fēng, bō làng zì qǐ

情海无风，波浪自起。

情海無風，波浪自起。

The sea of love itself is calm, the turbulence is generated by the individuals.

qíng rén yǎn lǐ chū xī shī

情人眼里出西施。

情人眼裡出西施。

Beauty is in the eye of the beholder.

qǐng jiào bié rén bù chī kuī

请教别人不吃亏。

請教別人不吃虧。

There is no disadvantage to asking for advice.

qióng bù kě qī, fù bù kě chí

穷不可欺，富不可持。

窮不可欺，富不可持。

Do not take advantage of the poor, and do not rely on the rich.

qióng rén de hái zi zǎo dāng jiā

穷人的孩子早当家。

窮人的孩子早當家。

Children of poor families take charge of the household at an early age.

qióng zé biàn, biàn zé tōng

穷则变，变则通。

窮則變，變則通。

An impasse is followed by change, and change will lead to a solution.

qióng zé dú shàn qí shēn, dá zé jiān shàn tiān xià

穷则独善其身,达则兼善天下。

窮則獨善其身,達則兼善天下。

When poor, you take care of yourself; when well-to-do, you take care of everyone.

qiú rén bù rú qiú jǐ

求人不如求己。

求人不如求己。

Better to help yourself than to ask for help from others.

qiú shén bù rú qiú rén

求神不如求人。

求神不如求人。

Better to ask a favor from others than from a god.

qǔ gāo hé guǎ

曲高和寡。

曲高和寡。

With high-brow songs, very few people join in the chorus.

qǔ ge xí fù fēn ge jiā

娶个媳妇分个家。

娶個媳婦分個家。

Take a wife and break up a family.

qǔ le xí fù wàng le niáng

娶了媳妇望了娘。

娶了媳婦望了娘。

Take a wife and you will forget about your mother.

qǔ qī qiú shú nǚ

娶妻求淑女。

娶妻求淑女。

For a wife, seek a lady.

qǔ qī qǔ dé bù qǔ sè

娶妻娶德不娶色。

娶妻娶德不娶色。

Marry a woman for her virtue, not for her looks.

qǔ rén zhī cháng, bǔ jǐ zhī duǎn

取人之长, 补己之短。

取人之長, 補己之短。

Overcome one's weakness by learning from other's strengths.

quán bù lí shǒu, qǔ bù lí kǒu

拳不离手, 曲不离口。

拳不離手, 曲不離口。

Boxers must practice boxing every day, and singers must practice singing every day.

Practice makes perfect.

R

ráo rén shì fú
饶人是福。
饒人是福。
A pardon produces good fortune.

rè jí shēng fēng
热极生风。
熱極生風。
Extreme heat produces wind.

rén bǐ rén, qì sǐ rén
人比人，气死人。
人比人，氣死人。
Comparisons are odious.

rén bú zài dà xiǎo, mǎ bú zài gāo dī
人不在大小，马不在高低。
人不在大小，馬不在高低。
Men are not judged by their size, and horses are not judged by their height.

rén bù kě mào xiàng, hǎi shuǐ bù kě dǒu liáng

人不可貌相，海水不可斗量。

人不可貌相，海水不可斗量。

You can't judge a person by his appearance, and you can't measure the sea with a bushel.

Great minds cannot be fathomed by ordinary minds.

rén bù qiú rén yì bān dà

人不求人一般大。

人不求人一般大。

If you don't beg others, you are on an equal footing.

rén bù xué, bù zhī yì

人不学，不知义。

人不學，不知義。

One must study to know what is righteous.

rén bù zhī jǐ chǒu, mǎ bù zhī liǎn cháng

人不知己丑，马不知脸长。

人不知己醜，馬不知臉長。

Man does not see his own ugliness, and horses are unaware of the length of their heads.

rén dào wú qiú pǐn zì gāo

人到无求品自高。

人到無求品自高。

One with no desires has an exalted character.

rén dào zhōng nián wàn shì yōu

人到中年万事忧。

人到中年萬事憂。

When people reach middle-age, they tend to worry a lot.

rén dìng shèng tiān

人定胜天。

人定勝天。

Man will triumph over nature.

rén duō hǎo bàn shì, chái duō hǎo qǔ nuǎn

人多好办事，柴多好取暖。

人多好辦事，柴多好取暖。

It is easier to handle affairs with more people, and it is easier to keep warm with more firewood.

rén duō zuǐ zá

人多嘴杂。

人多嘴雜。

Agreement is difficult when there are too many people involved.

rén ěr wú xìn, bù zhī qí kě

人而无信，不知其可？

人而無信，不知其可？

If a man does not keep his word, what good is he?

rén fēi cǎo mù, shú néng wú qíng

人非草木, 孰能无情?

人非草木, 孰能無情?

Men are not plants, how can they not have feelings?

rén fēi shēng ér zhī zhī, nǎi xué ér zhī zhī

人非生而知之, 乃学而知之。

人非生而知之, 乃學而知之。

At birth, we know nothing, and knowledge comes from learning.

rén fēi shèng xián, shú néng wú guò

人非圣贤, 孰能无过?

人非聖賢, 孰能無過?

Men are not saints, how can they be free from faults?

rén féng xǐ shì jīng shén shuǎng, yuè dào zhōng qiū fèn wài míng

人逢喜事精神爽, 月到中秋分外明。

人逢喜事精神爽, 月到中秋分外明。

Joy gives heart to a man, and the autumn moon seems especially bright.

rén gè yǒu suǒ hào

人各有所好。

人各有所好。

Every man has his preference.

rén guì yǒu zhì, xué guì yǒu héng

人贵有志, 学贵有恒。

人貴有志, 學貴有恆。

High aspirations are essential for a man as persistence is essential for learning.

rén guò liú míng, yàn guò liú shēng

人过留名, 雁过留声。

人過留名, 雁過留聲。

A person leaves behind his name as a goose leaves behind its call.

rén huì biàn, yuè huì yuán

人会变, 月会圆。

人會變, 月會圓。

People change as the moon waxes.

rén jí bàn bù liǎo shì, māo jí dǎo bú dào lǎo shǔ

人急办不了好事, 猫急逮不到老鼠。

人急辦不了好事, 貓急逮不到老鼠。

Men who are impatient cannot handle affairs well, and cats which are impatient cannot catch a mouse.

rén lǎo zhū huáng bù zhí qián

人老珠黄不值钱。

人老珠黃不值錢。

When people get old, they are like pearls with faded luster and they are no longer held in high esteem.

rén pà chū míng, zhū pà pàng

人怕出名, 猪怕胖。

人怕出名, 豬怕胖。

As fattening portends trouble for pigs, fame portends trouble for a man.

rén pèi yī fú, mǎ pèi ān

人配衣服, 马配鞍。

人配衣服, 馬配鞍。

Men are fitted with clothes, and horses are fitted with saddles.

rén píng bù yǔ, shuǐ píng bù liú

人平不语, 水平不流。

人平不語, 水平不流。

When there is no discontent, there will be no complaints, and on a flat surface, water will not flow.

rén píng zhì qì, hǔ píng wēi

人凭志气, 虎凭威。

人憑志氣, 虎憑威。

Men rely on aspirations as tigers rely on strength.

rén qín dì bù lǎn

人勤地不懒。

人勤地不懶。

Where the tiller is diligent, the land is busy.

rén qín dì shēng bǎo, rén lǎn dì shēng cǎo

人勤地生宝，人懒地生草。

人勤地生寶，人懶地生草。

The diligent grow treasures in the field, but the lazy grow weeds.

rén qióng zhì duǎn

人穷志短。

人窮志短。

Poverty stifles ambition.

rén shàn bèi rén qī, mǎ shàn bèi rén qí

人善被人欺，马善被人骑。

人善被人欺，馬善被人騎。

The good person will be taken advantage of by others as the tame horse will be ridden.

rén shēng qī shí cái kāi shǐ

人生七十才开始。

人生七十才開始。

Life begins at seventy.

rén shēng wú zhì, rú wú duò zhī zhōu

人生无志，如无舵之舟。

人生無志，如無舵之舟。

Life without aspirations is like a boat without a helm.

rén shēng zuì kǔ lǎo lái gū

人生最苦老来孤。

人生最苦老來孤。

Loneliness in old age is the worst bitterness in life.

rén tóng xīn, tǔ biàn jīn

人同心, 土变金。

人同心, 土變金。

A meeting of minds can turn dirt into gold.

rén wài yǒu rén, shān wài yǒu shān

人外有人, 山外有山。

人外有人, 山外有山。

However strong you are, there is always someone stronger.

rén wǎng dà chù kàn, niǎo wǎng gāo chù fēi

人往大处看, 鸟往高处飞。

人往大處看, 鳥往高處飛。

Men look at the overall picture, and birds fly toward high places.

rén wǎng gāo chù pá, shuǐ wǎng dī chù liú

人往高处爬, 水往地处流。

人往高處爬, 水往地處流。

Men seek high places, and water seeks low places.

rén wèi cái sǐ, niǎo wèi shí wáng

人为财死, 鸟为食亡。

人為財死, 鳥為食亡。

Men die for money, and birds die for food.

rén wú lián chǐ, bǎi shì kě wéi

人无廉耻, 百事可为。

人無廉恥, 百事可為。

If a man is impervious to shame, he can do all sorts of evil.

rén wú xiào liǎn bù kāi diàn

人无笑脸不开店。

人無笑臉不開店。

Don't go into business if you don't have a smiling face.

rén wú yuǎn lǜ, bì yǒu jìn yōu

人无远虑, 必有近忧。

人無遠慮, 必有近憂。

If a man makes no provisions for the distant future, he will certainly encounter difficulties in the near future.

rén xián shēng bìng, shí xián shēng tāi

人闲生病, 石闲生苔。

人閒生病, 石閒生苔。

Sickness visits the idle man as moss grows on the embedded stone.

rén xīn bù zú shé tūn xiàng

人心不足蛇吞象。

人心不足蛇吞象。

Greedy people are like snakes trying to swallow an elephant.

rén xīn gāo guò tiān, zuò le huáng dì xiǎng chéng xiān

人心高过天, 做了皇帝想成仙。

人心高過天, 做了皇帝想成仙。

Desires are insatiable - ascend the throne as emperor and you'll set your sights on immortality.

rén xīn nán mō

人心难摸。

人心難摸。

The human heart is difficult to grasp.

rén xīn yào gōng, huǒ xīn yào kōng

人心要公, 火心要空。

人心要公, 火心要空。

As the center of a fire needs space, a person's heart needs to be fair.

rén xīn zhuān, shí shān chuān

人心专, 石山穿。

人心專, 石山穿。

Maintain focus and you can bore through a mountain.

rén xíng qiān lǐ lù, shèng dú shí nián shū

人行千里路, 胜读十年书。

人行千里路, 勝讀十年書。

One benefits more from taking a trip than from 10 years of study.

rén yào cháng jiāo, zhàng zhài yào duǎn jié

人要长交, 账要短结。

人要長交, 賬要短結。

Friendship should be long-lived while debts should be short-lived.

rén yào chuǎng, mǎ yào fàng

人要闯, 马要放。

人要闖, 馬要放。

Men should venture out into the world, and horses should venture out to graze.

rén yào liǎn, shù yào pí

人要脸, 树要皮。

人要臉, 樹要皮。

Face is as important to man as bark is to the tree.

rén yào yī zhuāng, fó yào jīn zhuāng

人要衣装, 佛要金装。

人要衣装, 佛要金装。

Men dress up with clothes, and the Buddha dresses up with gold.

rén yǒu héng xīn, wàn shì chéng

人有恒心，万事成。

人有恆心，萬事成。

With perseverance, one can achieve many things.

rén yǒu zhì, zhú yǒu jié

人有志，竹有节。

人有志，竹有節。

Men have aspirations as bamboo has joints.

rén zài ǎi yán xià, bù kě bù dī tóu

人在矮檐下，不可不低头。

人在矮簷下，不可不低頭。

If you are standing under low eaves, you must duck your head.

Those who serve must remain subordinant.

rén zài shì shàng liàn, dāo zài shí shàng mó

人在世上炼，刀在石上磨。

人在世上煉，刀在石上磨。

The world refines a man as a stone sharpens a knife.

rén zhě jiàn rén, zhì zhě jiàn zhì

仁者见仁，智者见智。

仁者見仁，智者見智。

The benevolent see benevolence, and the wise see wisdom.

Different people have different points of view.

rén zhēng qì, huǒ zhēng yàn

人争气，火争焰。

人爭氣，火爭焰。

People strive for high spirits as fire strives to become flames.

rén zhēng yì kǒu qì, fó zhēng yí zhù xiāng

人争一口气，佛争一柱香。

人爭一口氣，佛爭一柱香。

Men strive for vindication while God strives for manifestation.

rén zhī xiāng zhī, guì zài zhī xīn

人之相知，贵在知心。

人之相知，貴在知心。

The most important thing in knowing another is to know what lies in the heart.

rén zhuàn qián nán, qián zhuàn qián róng yì

人赚钱难，钱赚钱容易。

人賺錢難，錢賺錢容易。

It is easy for money to make money, but it's hard for man to make money.

rén zuǐ rú qīng cǎo, fēng chuī liǎng biān dǎo

人嘴如青草，风吹两边倒。

人嘴如青草，風吹兩邊倒。

Our mouths are like grass swaying with the prevailing wind.

rěn yì shí zhī nù, kě miǎn bǎi rì zhī yōu

忍一时之怒, 可免百日之忧。

忍一時之怒, 可免百日之憂。

Restrain yourself in a moment of anger, and you'll avoid long periods of sorrow.

rěn zì jiā zhōng bǎo

忍字家中宝。

忍字家中寶。

Tolerance is the treasure of the home.

rěn zuǐ bú qiàn zhài

忍嘴不欠债。

忍嘴不欠債。

If you limit your desires, you will avoid debts.

rì guāng bú zhào mén, yī shēng jiù shàng mén

日光不照门, 医生就上门。

日光不照門, 醫生就上門。

The home which sunlight never enters will be visited by the doctor.

rù jìng suí sú

入境随俗。

入境隨俗。

When in Rome do as the Romans do.

ruó néng kè gāng

柔能克刚。

柔能克剛。

Gentleness overcomes harshness.

ruò fēi yì fān hán chè gǔ, yān dé méi huā pū bí xiāng

若非一番寒彻骨，焉得梅花扑鼻香。

若非一番寒徹骨，焉得梅花撲鼻香。

Without the bitter cold of winter, how can one enjoy the fragrance of the plum blossoms?

ruò yào jiàn, tiān tiān liàn

若要健，天天练。

若要健，天天練。

If you want to be healthy, exercise every day.

ruò yào rén bù zhī, chú fēi jǐ mò wéi

若要人不知，除非己莫为。

若要人不知，除非己莫為。

The best way to not be caught is to not commit the act.

S

sān ge chòu pí jiàng, shèng guò yì ge zhū gě liàng

三个臭皮匠,胜过一个诸葛亮。

三個臭皮匠,勝過一個諸葛亮。

The wisdom of three shoemakers can exceed that of a wise man.

Two heads are better than one.

sān nián fēng shuǐ lún liú zhuǎn

三年风水轮流转。

三年風水輪流轉。

The fengshui rotates every three years.

Every dog has its day.

sān rén tóng xīn duó tiān xià

三人同心夺天下。

三人同心奪天下。

Three people of a common mind can conquer the world.

sān rén xíng bì yǒu wǒ shī

三人行必有我师。

三人行必有我師。

When I walk in a group of three, among the others I may find a teacher for me.

sān sī ěr hòu xíng
三思而后行。
三思而後行。
Look before you leap.

sān tiān bú niàn kǒu shēng, sān nián bú zuò shǒu shēng
三天不念口生, 三年不做手生。
三天不唸口生, 三年不做手生。
Fall behind in practice and your skills will fade.

shā lì suī xiǎo, shāng rén yǎn
沙粒虽小, 伤人眼。
沙粒雖小, 傷人眼。
Sand is minute, but it will harm your eyes.

shān dà yā bú zhù quán shuǐ , niú dà yā bù sǐ shī zi
山大压不住泉水, 牛大压不死虱子。
山大壓不住泉水, 牛大壓不死蝨子。
A big mountain can't stop spring water, and a large bull cannot kill lice.

shān yǔ yù lái fēng mǎn lóu
山雨欲来风满楼。
山雨欲來風滿樓。
A turbulent wind precedes the mountain storm.

shàn bù jī, bù zú yǐ chéng míng

善不积, 不足以成名。

善不積, 不足以成名。

If you don't do good deeds, you will not build a good reputation.

shàn è bù tóng tú, bīng tàn bù tóng lú

善恶不同途, 冰炭不同炉。

善惡不同途, 冰炭不同爐。

Good and evil follow different paths as ice and coal come from different sources.

shàn è dào tóu zhōng yǒu bào, yuǎn zǒu gāo fēi yě nán táo

善恶到头终有报, 远走高飞也难逃。

善惡到頭終有報, 遠走高飛也難逃。

Good and bad ultimately lead to inescapable consequences.

shàn shǐ zé gōng jìn yú chéng

善始则功近于成。

善始則功近于成。

Well begun is half done.

shàn yǒu shàn bào, è yǒu è bào

善有善报, 恶有恶报。

善有善報, 惡有惡報。

Good has its reward and evil has its cost.

shàng liáng bú zhèng, xià liáng wāi

上梁不正，下梁歪。

上樑不正，下樑歪。

If the upper beam is not straight, the lower ones will be crooked.

shàng shān qín hǔ yì, kāi kǒu qiú rén nán

上山擒虎易，开口求人难。

上山擒虎易，開口求人難。

It's easier to catch a tiger on a mountain than to beg for help.

shǎo chī duō zī wèi, duō chī huó shòu zuì

少吃多滋味，多吃活受罪。

少吃多滋味，多吃活受罪。

Eat less and enjoy the taste more, eat more and enjoy your health less.

shào nián bù zhī qín xué zǎo, bái tóu fāng huǐ dú shū chí

少年不知勤学早，白头方悔读书迟。

少年不知勤學早，白頭方悔讀書遲。

Study hard when you are young or you'll regret it when you are old.

shào zhuàng bù nǔ lì, lǎo dà tú shāng bēi

少壮不努力，老大徒伤悲。

少壯不努力，老大徒傷悲。

Laziness in youth spells regret in old age.

shē zhě fù bù zú, jiǎn zhě pín yǒu yú

奢者富不足, 俭者贫有余。

奢者富不足, 儉者貧有餘。

No matter how rich, the extravagant never have enough; no matter how poor, the thrifty always have enough.

shé cháng shì duō, yè cháng mèng duō

舌长事多, 夜长梦多。

舌長事多, 夜長夢多。

With a long tongue, affairs will multiply; over a long night, dreams will multiply.

shé jiàn lì yú dāo jiàn

舌剑利于刀剑。

舌劍利於刀劍。

The tongue cuts deeper than the sword.

shé tóu shì ròu zhǎng de, shì shí shì tiě dǎ de

舌头是肉长的, 事实是铁打的。

舌頭是肉長的, 事實是鐵打的。

The tongue grows out of the flesh and facts are cast from iron.

shēn jiào shèng yú yán jiào

身教胜于言教。

身教勝于言教。

An example is better than a precept.

shēn zài fú zhōng bù zhī fú

身在福中不知福。

身在福中不知福。

When we are happy, we aren't aware we are happy.

shēn zhèng bú pà yǐng ér xié

身正不怕影儿斜。

身正不怕影兒斜。

The upright man is not concerned that his shadow is crooked.

shěn qí wéi rén, guān qí zhū fǎn

审其为人, 观其诸反。

審其為人, 觀其諸反。

If you want to know someone's character, look at the friends he keeps.

shēng ēn bù rú yǎng ēn

生恩不如养恩。

生恩不如養恩。

The gratitude for raising a child is greater than that for giving birth to one.

shēng lǎo bìng sǐ, rén zhī cháng qíng

生老病死, 人之常情。

生老病死, 人之常情。

Birth, aging, sickness, and death - such is the lot of every man.

shēng yǒu yá ěr zhī wú yá

生有涯而知无涯。

生有涯而知無涯。

Life is limited, but knowledge is unlimited.

shēng yú yōu huàn, sǐ yú ān lè

生于忧患, 死于安乐。

生於憂患, 死於安樂。

Life springs from sorrow and calamity; death results from ease and pleasure.

shèng bài nǎi bīng jiā cháng shì

胜败乃兵家常事。

勝敗乃兵家常事。

For a military commander, victory and defeat are common occurrences.

shèng bù jiāo, bài bù něi

胜不骄, 败不馁。

勝不驕, 敗不餒。

Do not become dizzy with success or disheartened by failure.

shèng nù zhī xià shì wéi rén

盛怒之下识为人。

盛怒之下識為人。

True character is revealed in moments of extreme anger.

shī bài shì chéng gōng zhī mǔ

失败是成功之母。

失敗是成功之母。

Failure is the mother of success.

shī bǐ shòu yǒu fú

施比受有福。

施比受有福。

To give is more blessed than to receive.

shī luò cùn jīn róng yì zhǎo, cuò guò guāng yīn wú chù xún

失落寸金容易找, 错过光阴无处寻。

失落寸金容易找, 錯過光陰無處尋。

A lost bit of gold may be found, but not lost time.

shí bù qióng, chuān bù qióng, bú huì dǎ suàn yí shì qióng

食不穷, 穿不穷, 不会打算一世穷。

食不窮, 穿不窮, 不會打算一世窮。

You don't eat or clothe yourself into the poorhouse, but when
you can't keep a budget, you will be forever poor.

shí ge méi pó jiǔ ge huǎng

十个媒婆九个谎。

十個媒婆九個謊。

Nine out of ten matchmakers are liars.

shí lǎo jiǔ bìng

十老九病。

十老九病。

Old age brings illness.

shí nián shù mù, bǎi nián shù rén

十年树木, 百年树人。

十年樹木, 百年樹人。

It takes ten years to grow a tree, and one hundred years for a
sound educational program to take root.

shí shì bàn tōng, bù rú yí yì jīng tōng

十事半通, 不如一艺精通。

十事半通, 不如一藝精通。

Better a master of one field than a dilettante in ten.

shí shì zào yīng xióng

时势造英雄。

時勢造英雄。

Every age will produce its own heroes.

shì bù jīng bù dǒng, lù bù zǒu bù píng

事不经不懂, 路不走不平。

事不經不懂, 路不走不平。

You can't understand what you have not experienced, as the
unused road will not be smoothened.

shì chéng yú hé mù, lì shēng yú tuán jié

事成于和睦, 力生于团结。

事成於和睦, 力生於團結。

Undertakings succeed from harmony, and strength results from unity.

shì fēi jīng guò bù zhī nán

事非经过不知难。

事非經過不知難。

One does not realized the difficulty of an undertaking unless he has experienced it before.

shì fēi nán táo zhòng kǒu

是非难逃众口。

是非難逃眾口。

Public opinion is the arbiter of right and wrong.

shì fēi zhōng rì yǒu, bù tīng zì rán wú

是非终日有, 不听自然无。

是非終日有, 不聽自然無。

Gossip may abound, but if you don't listen to it, there will be no gossip.

shì fēi zì yǒu gōng lùn

是非自有公论。

是非自有公論。

The masses decide what is right and wrong.

shì kě shā, bù kě rù

士可杀, 不可辱。

士可殺, 不可辱。

A brave man can be killed but not dishonored.

shì shí shèng yú xióng biàn

事实胜于雄辩。

事實勝於雄辯。

Facts speak louder than words.

shì shí wù zhě wéi jùn jié

识时务者为俊杰。

識時務者為俊傑。

He who comprehends the times is a great man.

shì suī xiǎo, bú zuò bù chéng; zǐ sūn xián, bù jiāo bù míng

事虽小, 不做不成; 子孙贤, 不教不明。

事雖小, 不做不成; 子孫賢, 不教不明。

Even the simplest undertaking requires effort before it can be completed; even the ablest child must receive instruction to become intelligent.

shǒu pà bú dòng, nǎo pà bú yòng

手怕不动, 脑怕不用。

手怕不動, 腦怕不用。

With hands, be concerned about not working with them; with the brain, be concerned about not using it.

shū dào yòng shí fāng hèn shǎo

书到用时方恨少。

書到用時方恨少。

When the time comes to apply our knowledge, we regret not having it.

shū dú bǎi bian, qí yì zì míng

书读百遍, 其义自明。

書讀百遍, 其義自明。

Read a book one hundred times and its meaning will become clear.

shū shān yǒu lù qín wéi jìng

书山有路勤为径。

書山有路勤為徑。

Diligence is the path to learning.

shú néng shēng qiǎo

熟能生巧。

熟能生巧。

Practice makes perfect.

shú shuǐ xìng, hǎo huá chuán

熟水性, 好划船。

熟水性, 好划船。

If you are familiar with the nature of water, it is easier to row a boat.

shù dà zhāo fēng

树大招风。

樹大招風。

A tall tree catches the wind.

Persons in high places are more likely to attract attention.

shù gāo qiān zhàng, yè luò guī gēn

树高千丈, 叶落归根。

樹高千丈, 葉落歸根。

A tree may grow tall but its leaves still fall back down to the roots.

shù kào gēn, wū kào liáng

树靠根, 屋靠梁。

樹靠根, 屋靠樑。

As roots are essential for a tree, beams are essential for a house.

shù kào rén xiū, rén kào zì xiū

树靠人修, 人靠自修。

樹靠人修, 人靠自修。

Trees are trimmed by man, while man improves himself through study.

shù lǎo bàn xīn kōng, rén lǎo bǎi shì tōng

树老半心空, 人老百事通。

樹老半心空, 人老百事通。

Old trees are hollow, but old men are knowledgeable about many things.

shù lǎo gēn duō, rén lǎo shì duō

树老根多, 人老识多。

樹老根多, 人老識多。

As an old tree has many roots, an old person has much knowledge.

shù pà bō pí, rén pà shāng xīn

树怕剥皮, 人怕伤心。

樹怕剝皮, 人怕傷心。

People fear a broken heart as a tree fears peeling bark.

shù xiǎo fú zhí yì, shù dà fú zhí nán

树小扶直易, 树大扶直难。

樹小扶直易, 樹大扶直難。

It is easy to straighten out a small tree, but not so a large tree.

shuǐ bù liú huì chòu, miáo bù guǎn méi shōu

水不流会臭, 苗不管没收。

水不流會臭, 苗不管沒收。

Stagnant water stinks, and untended seedlings produce no crops.

shuǐ huǒ wú qíng

水火无情。

水火無情。

Floods and fire have no mercy.

shuǐ qiǎn bù róng dà zhōu

水浅不容大舟。

水淺不容大舟。

Shallow water will not support a large boat.

shuǐ shēn bù xiǎng, xiǎng shuǐ bù shēn

水深不响, 响水不深。

水深不響, 響水不深。

Deep water is silent and noisy water is not deep.

shuǐ shēn liú qù màn, zhì rén huà yǔ chí

水深流去慢, 智人话语迟。

水深流去慢, 智人話語遲。

Deep water flows slowly, and wise men measure their words.

shuǐ suī píng, yì yǒu bō; héng suī zhǔn, yì yǒu chā

水虽平, 亦有波；衡虽准, 亦有差。

水雖平, 亦有波；衡雖準亦有差。

Calm water also produces waves, and the calibrated scale will also be slightly off.

shuǐ yǒu yuán, shù yǒu gēn

水有源, 树有根。

水有源, 樹有根。

Water has its source, and trees have their roots.

shuǐ zhì qīng, zé wú yú

水至清，则无鱼。

水至清，則無魚。

You won't find fish in clear water.

shùn fēng chuī huǒ, yòng lì bù duō

顺风吹火，用力不多。

順風吹火，用力不多。

Blow on the fire with the wind at your back and you'll expend less effort.

sī zhōng yǒu guò, máng zhōng yǒu cuò

私中有过，忙中有错。

私中有過，忙中有錯。

Selfishness and haste produce mistakes.

sì hǎi zhī nèi jiē xiōng dì

四海之内皆兄弟。

四海之內皆兄弟。

All men are brothers.

sì zǐ qiān jīn, bù rú sì zǐ yí yì

赐子千金，不如赐子一艺。

賜子千金，不如賜子一藝。

Better to impart a single skill upon a child than to bestow upon the child a thousand pieces of gold.

suì yuè bù ráo rén

岁月不饶人。

歲月不饒人。

Time spares no one.

suì yuè tiān rén shòu, bēi chóu cuī rén lǎo

岁月添人寿, 悲愁催人老。

歲月添人壽, 悲愁催人老。

Time adds to your longevity, and sorrow adds to your old age.

T

tā shān zhī shí, kě yǐ gōng cuò

他山之石, 可以攻错。

他山之石, 可以攻錯。

A good quality of another may provide the remedy for our faults.

tān duō jiǎo bú làn

贪多嚼不烂。

貪多嚼不爛。

If you stuff your mouth full, you can't chew thoroughly.

tān shí yú ér yì shàng gōu

贪食鱼儿易上钩。

貪食魚兒易上鈎。

The fish that nibbles at every lure will soon be caught.

tān zhě bì shī

贪者必失。

貪者必失。

Those who are greedy will lose in the end.

tǐ zhuàng rén qī bìng, tǐ ruò rén bìng qī

体壮人欺病, 体弱人病欺。

體壯人欺病, 體弱人病欺。

The strong ward off disease while the weak are strickened by it.

tiān bù shēng wú yòng zhī rén, dì bù zhǎng wú míng zhī cǎo

天不生无用之人, 地不长无名之草。

天不生無用之人, 地不長無名之草。

There are no useless people as there are no plants without a name.

tiān bù yán zì gāo, dì bù yán zì hòu

天不言自高, 地不言自厚。

天不言自高, 地不言自厚。

Heaven does not refer to its height, and the earth does not refer to its breadth.

tiān cái zài yú qín fèn

天才在于勤奋。

天才在於勤奮。

Genius comes from diligence.

tiān lěng bú dòng máng rén

天冷不冻忙人。

天冷不凍忙人。

Cold weather does not chill a busy person.

tiān qíng bù kāi gōu, yǔ luò biàn dì liú

天晴不开沟, 雨落遍地流。

天晴不開溝, 雨落遍地流。

Dig a ditch while the sky is clear, or you'll have flooding when it rains.

tiān shēng wǒ cái bì yǒu yòng

天生我材必有用。

天生我材必有用。

Every life has a purpose.

tiān tiān bù fā chóu, huó dào bǎi chū tóu

天天不发愁, 活到百出头。

天天不發愁, 活到百出頭。

Avoid worry each day and live to a ripe old age.

tiān wǎng huī huī, shū ěr bú lòu

天网恢恢, 疏而不漏。

天網恢恢, 疏而不漏。

God's mill grinds slowly but surely.

tiān wú jué rén zhī lù

天无绝人之路。

天無絕人之路。

There is always a way out.

tiān xià wū yā yì bān huī

天下乌鸦一般黑。

天下烏鴉一般黑。

All crows are black.

Evil is the same everywhere.

tiān xià wú bú sàn de yàn xí

天下无不散的宴席。

天下無不散的宴席。

There is an end to every party.

All good things come to an end.

tiān xià wú bú shì de fù mǔ

天下无不是的父母。

天下無不是的父母。

No parent is ever wrong.

tiān xià wú nán shì, zhǐ pà yǒu xīn rén

天下无难事, 只怕有心人。

天下無難事, 祇怕有心人。

Where there is a will, there is a way.

tiān xià wú yún bú xià yǔ, shì jiān wú lǐ shì bù chéng

天下无云不下雨, 世间无理事不成。

天下無雲不下雨, 世間無理事不成。

No clouds, no rain; no rules, no gain.

tiān yǒu bú cè fēng yún, rén yǒu dàn xì huò fú

天有不测风云，人有旦夕祸福。

天有不測風雲，人有旦夕禍福。

In nature, there are unexpected storms; in life, there are unexpected outcomes.

tiān yǒu hán shǔ yīn qíng, rén yǒu bēi huān lí hé

天有寒暑阴晴，人有悲欢离合。

天有寒暑陰晴，人有悲歡離合。

In nature, there are cold, hot, cloudy, and clear days; in life, there is sorrow, joy, separation, and unity.

tiān yǒu hào shēng zhī dé

天有好生之德。

天有好生之德。

Heaven provides a means for everything.

tiān zhù zì zhù zhě

天助自助者。

天助自助者。

Heaven helps those who help themselves.

tīng guò bù rú jiàn guò, jiàn guò bù rú zuò guò

听过不如见过，见过不如做过。

聽過不如見過，見過不如做過。

Better to see it than to hear it, and better to do it than to see it.

tīng xiǎo huà, wù dà shì

听小话，误大事。

聽小話，誤大事。

Listen to idle talk and doom great plans.

tóng háng shì yuān jiā

同行是冤家。

同行是冤家。

Two persons in the same trade will never agree.

tóng háng xiāng jì

同行相嫉。

同行相嫉。

Those in the same trade contend with each other.

tóng shēng xiāng yìng, tóng qì xiāng qiú

同声相应，同气相求。

同聲相應，同氣相求。

Like attracts like.

tōu ge jī dàn chī bù bǎo, yì shēn chòu míng bēi dào lǎo

偷个鸡蛋吃不饱，一身臭名背到老。

偷個雞蛋吃不飽，一身臭名背到老。

You can't fill your stomach with a single stolen egg, but a bad reputation will follow you into old age.

tóu huí shàng dàng, èr huí xīn liàng

头回上当, 二回心亮。

頭回上當, 二回心亮。

Once bitten, twice shy.

tù zi bù chī wō biān cǎo

兔子不吃窝边草。

兔子不吃窩邊草。

A rabbit does not eat the grass near its own hole.
Even a scoundrel doesn't harm his neighbor.

tuán jié jiù shì lì liàng

团结就是力量。

團結就是力量。

Unity is strength.

tuán jié lì liàng dà, chái duō huǒ yàn gāo

团结力量大, 柴多火焰高。

團結力量大, 柴多火焰高。

In unity, there is strength, just as many pieces of wood create
a large fire.

tuán jié yì tiáo xīn, huáng tǔ biàn huáng jīn

团结一条心, 黄土变黄金。

團結一條心, 黃土變黃金。

Unity can turn dirt into gold.

W

wài lái de hé shàng huì niàn jīng

外来的和尚会念经。

外來的和尚會唸經。

Foreign monks recite scriptures better.

The grass is always greener on the other side of the fence.

wài mào róng yì rèn, nèi xīn zuì nán cāi

外貌容易认，内心最难猜。

外貌容易認，內心最難猜。

It's easy to recognize appearances, but difficult to fathom the mind.

wàn bān jiē xià pǐn, wěi yǒu dú shū gāo

万般皆下品，唯有读书高。

萬般皆下品，唯有讀書高。

Among all pursuits, study is the best.

wàn è jiē yóu zì sī qǐ

万恶皆由自私起。

萬惡皆由自私起。

Selfishness is the root of all evil.

wàn shì qǐ tóu nán, zuò le jiù bù nán

万事起头难, 做了就不难。

萬事起頭難, 做了就不難。

Everything is hard in the beginning and gets easier once underway.

wàn wù shēng yú tǔ, wàn wù guī yú tǔ

万物生于土, 万物归于土。

萬物生於土, 萬物歸於土。

All things arise from the earth and return to the earth.

Ashes to ashes and dust to dust.

wàn zhàng gāo lóu píng dì qǐ

万丈高楼平地起。

萬丈高樓平地起。

Tall buildings rise up from the ground.

wáng yáng bǔ láo, yóu wèi wéi wǎn

亡羊补牢, 犹未为晚。

亡羊補牢, 猶未為晚。

Even if some of the sheep have escaped, it is still not too late to fix the fence.

Better late than never.

wáng zǐ fàn fǎ, yǔ mín tóng zuì

王子犯法, 与民同罪。

王子犯法, 與民同罪。

When the prince breaks the law, he should be punished like everyone else.

wéi rén bú pà cuò, jiù pà bù gǎi guò

为人不怕错，就怕不改过。

為人不怕錯，就怕不改過。

Fear not mistakes, but fear repeating them.

wéi rén bù dāng tóu, wéi mù bù dāng zhú

为人不当头，为木不当轴。

為人不當頭，為木不當軸。

Keep out of the spotlight.

wéi shàn cháng lè

为善常乐。

為善常樂。

The pleasure of doing good deeds never wears out.

wén jī qǐ wǔ, bǎi shì jù xīng

闻鸡起舞，百事俱兴。

聞雞起舞，百事俱興。

Start your day early and everything will prosper.

wén xì kào zuǐ, wǔ xì kào tuǐ

文戏靠嘴，武戏靠腿。

文戲靠嘴，武戲靠腿。

Drama depends on the mouth while martial arts depend on the legs.

wěn jiàn zhā shí bì zhì shèng

稳健扎实必致胜。

穩健紮實必致勝。

Slow and steady wins the race.

wèn biàn wàn jiā chéng háng jiā

问遍万家成行家。

問遍萬家成行家。

Ask around and you'll become an expert.

wèn lù bù shī lǐ, duō zǒu èr shí lǐ

问路不施礼, 多走二十里。

問路不施禮, 多走二十里。

If you are not polite when you ask for directions, you may end up going an extra twenty miles.

wū yā bào xǐ méi rén xìn

乌鸦报喜没人信。

烏鴉報喜沒人信。

No one believes it when a crow bears good news.

wū yā bù yǔ fèng huáng qī

乌鸦不与凤凰栖。

烏鴉不與鳳凰棲。

The crow doesn't perch on the same branch as the phoenix.

wú chǒu bù chéng xì

无丑不成戏。

無丑不成戲。

Every drama requires a clown.

wú fēng bù qǐ làng

无风不起浪。

無風不起浪。

Where there's smoke, there's fire.

wú gōng bú shòu lù

无功不受禄。

無功不受祿。

No reward without good deeds.

wú guān yì shēn qīng

无官一身轻。

無官一身輕。

Avoid officialdom and your life will be carefree.

wú jiān bù xiǎn zhōng

无奸不显忠。

無奸不顯忠。

Without traitors, the loyal do not stand out.

wú qián bù chéng shì

无钱不成事。

無錢不成事。

Things don't get done without money.

wú qiǎo bù chéng shū

无巧不成书。

無巧不成書。

There is no story without coincidences.

wú shì xián rì cháng, yǒu shì xián rì duǎn

无事嫌日长, 有事嫌日短。

無事嫌日長, 有事嫌日短。

When you are bored, time drags on, but when you are busy, the days are short.

wú zhài yì shēn qīng

无债一身轻。

無債一身輕。

Avoid debt and your life will be carefree.

wú zhēn bù yǐn xiàn, wú shuǐ bù xíng chuán

无针不引线, 无水不行船。

無針不引線, 無水不行船。

You don't pull without a needle, and you don't row a boat without water.

wǔ shí bù xiào bǎi bù

五十步笑百步。

五十步笑百步。

Fifty steps laugh at one hundred steps.
The pot calls the kettle black.

wù jí bì fǎn

物极必反。

物極必反。

The pendulum always swings back.

wù tān yì wài zhī cái

勿贪意外之财。

勿貪意外之財。

Don't covet unexpected fortune.

wù yào fáng làn, rén yào fáng lǎn

物要防烂，人要防懒。

物要防爛，人要防懶。

Guard goods against rotting; guard people against laziness.

wù yǐ lèi jù

物以类聚。

物以類聚。

Birds of a feather flock together.

wù yǐ xī wéi guì

物以稀为贵。

物以稀為貴。

The thing which is rare is dear.

X

xí guàn chéng zì rán

习惯成自然。

習慣成自然。

Habits become second-nature.

xí huā huā jiē guǒ, ài liǔ liǔ chéng yìn

惜花花结果, 爱柳柳成荫。

惜花花結果, 愛柳柳成蔭。

Love and attention make all things grow.

xì jiǎo màn yān, shòu huó bǎi nián

细嚼慢咽, 寿活百年。

細嚼慢嚥, 壽活百年。

Chewing carefully and swallowing slowly will make for a long life.

xiā zi jiàn qián yǎn yě kāi

瞎子见钱眼也开。

瞎子見錢眼也開。

Even a blind man opens his eyes when there is money.

xiān dān nán zhì méi liáng xīn

仙丹难治没良心。

仙丹難治沒良心。

Even the elixir of life cannot cure one without a conscience.

xiān kǔ hòu gān, fù guì wàn nián

先苦后甘, 富贵万年。

先苦後甘, 富貴萬年。

Taste bitter before sweet and enjoy years of good fortune.

xiān xià shǒu wéi qiáng, hòu xià shǒu zāo yāng

先下手为强, 后下手遭殃。

先下手為強, 後下手遭殃。

Strike first and prevail, strike late and fail.

xiāng huā bù yí dìng hǎo kàn, huì shuō bù yí dìng néng gàn

香花不一定好看, 会说不一定能干。

香花不一定好看, 會說不一定能幹。

Fragrant flowers are not necessarily beautiful, and eloquent speakers are not necessarily capable.

xiāng mà wú hǎo kǒu, xiāng dǎ wú hǎo shǒu

相骂无好口, 相打无好手。

相罵無好口, 相打無好手。

The good mouth doesn't curse and the good hand doesn't fight.

xiǎng yào guò hé xiān dā qiáo

想要过河先搭桥。

想要過河先搭橋。

If you want to cross the river, you must first build a bridge.

xiàng yáng fáng zi xiān dé nuǎn, kào shuǐ rén jiā huì chēng chuán

向阳房子先得暖, 靠水人家会撑船。

向陽房子先得暖, 靠水人家會撑船。

The house that faces the sun warms up first, and the person that lives near water knows how to row a boat.

xiǎo bié shèng xīn hūn

小别胜新婚。

小別勝新婚。

Reunion after a brief separation is better than a honeymoon.

xiǎo bù rěn zé luàn dà móu

小不忍则乱大谋。

小不忍則亂大謀。

He who cannot endure small defeats will fail at large tasks.

xiǎo cái bù chū, dà cái bú rù

小财不出, 大财不入。

小財不出, 大財不入。

You must invest a little to gain a lot.

xiǎo chuán bù yí zhòng zǎi

小船不宜重载。

小船不宜重載。

Small boats shouldn't carry large loads.

xiǎo ér wú zhà bìng

小儿无诈病。

小兒無詐病。

Small children do not deceive.

xiǎo hái bù néng guàn, yí guàn dìng yǒu luàn

小孩不能惯，一惯定有乱。

小孩不能慣，一慣定有亂。

You shouldn't spoil a child or it will certainly lead to trouble.

xiǎo hái zuǐ lǐ tǔ zhēn yán

小孩嘴里吐真言。

小孩嘴裡吐真言。

Children speak the truth.

xiǎo hé gōu yě néng fān chuán

小河沟也能翻船。

小河溝也能翻船。

Even a small stream can tip a boat.

xiǎo rén dé cùn biàn jìn chǐ

小人得寸便进尺。

小人得寸便進尺。

Give scoundrels an inch and they will take a yard.

xiǎo rén jì chóu, jūn zǐ gǎn ēn

小人记仇，君子感恩。

小人記仇，君子感恩。

The scoundrel recalls minor insults while the gentleman is filled with gratitude.

xiǎo rén wù, yì fā nù

小人物，易发怒。

小人物，易發怒。

The little pot is soonest hot.

xiǎo rén xián jū zuò dǎi shì

小人闲居做歹事。

小人閒居做歹事。

Idle hands are the devil's playground.

xiǎo rén xīn duō, ǎi shù gēn duō

小人心多，矮树根多。

小人心多，矮樹根多。

Scoundrels have many tricks up their sleeves just as short trees have many roots.

xiǎo rén zì dà, xiǎo xī shēng dà

小人自大，小溪声大。

小人自大，小溪聲大。

Scoundrels are arrogant just as little creeks make the most noise.

xiǎo shí bù zhī lǎo niáng qīn, yù ér cái zhī bào niáng ēn

小时不知老娘亲, 育儿才知报娘恩。

小時不知老娘親, 育兒才知報娘恩。

Children don't realize how good their mother is until they grow up and raise children of their own.

xiǎo shí liǎo liǎo, dà wèi bì jiā

小时了了, 大未必佳。

小時了了, 大未必佳。

Smart children do not necessarily grow into remarkable adults.

xiǎo shí tōu zhēn, dà le tōu jīn

小时偷针, 大了偷金。

小時偷針, 大了偷金。

One who steals a needle as a child will steal gold as an adult.

xiǎo xīn shǐ de wàn nián chuán

小心驶得万年船。

小心駛得萬年船。

With caution, one can sail a boat safely for ten thousand years.

xiǎo xīn tiān xià kě zǒu, lǔ mǎng cùn bù nán xíng

小心天下可走, 鲁莽寸步难行。

小心天下可走, 魯莽寸步難行。

Proceed with caution and travel everywhere; proceed recklessly and go nowhere.

xiǎo yǔ jiǔ xià néng chéng zāi

小雨久下能成災。

小雨久下能成灾。

Frequent drizzle can cause floods.

xiǎo zhì fáng dà diē

小踬防大跌。

小躓防大跌。

A stumble may prevent a fall.

xiào kǒu cháng kāi, qīng chūn cháng zài

笑口常开, 青春常在。

笑口常開, 青春常在。

Smile often and you will remain youthful.

xiào mén kāi, xìng fú lái

笑门开, 幸福来。

笑門開, 幸福來。

A sunny disposition brings good fortune.

xīn bú zhèng, xíng bù wěn

心不正, 行不稳。

心不正, 行不穩。

The man of low integrity travels a rocky road.

xīn guān shàng rèn sān bǎ huǒ

新官上任三把火。

新官上任三把火。

A new broom sweeps clean.

xīn huān fǎn shào nián

心欢返少年。

心歡返少年。

A joyous heart brings back youth.

xīn jí chī bù dé rè zhōu

心急吃不得热粥。

心急吃不得熱粥。

The impatient should not eat scalding hot gruel.

xīn jìng zì rán liáng

心静自然凉。

心靜自然涼。

When one is calm, one is cool.

xīn kuān bú pà fáng wū zǎi

心宽不怕房屋窄

心寬不怕房屋窄

With a broad mind, there is no fear of a narrow house.

xīn kuān tǐ pàng

心宽体胖。

心寬體胖。

Broad mind, ample body.

xīn lǐ tòng kuài bǎi bìng xiāo

心里痛快百病消。

心裡痛快百病消。

A joyous heart cures one hundred illnesses.

xīn zhèng bú pà xié

心正不怕邪。

心正不怕邪。

Evil will not harm a person of integrity.

xīn zhōng yǒu shéi, shéi jiù piào liàng

心中有谁, 谁就漂亮。

心中有誰, 誰就漂亮。

Whoever is in your heart is beautiful.

xīng jiā yóu rú zhēn tiāo tǔ, bài jiā hǎo sì shuǐ tuī zhōu

兴家犹如针挑土, 败家好似水推舟。

興家猶如針挑土, 敗家好似水推舟。

To bring prosperity to a family is as difficult as carrying dirt with a needle; to lead a family to ruin is as easy as casting a boat downstream.

xīng xīng zhī huǒ kě yǐ liáo yuán

星星之火可以燎原。

星星之火可以燎原。

A single spark can start a prairie fire.

xíng bǎi lǐ zhě bàn jiǔ shí

行百里者半九十。

行百里者半九十。

The going is toughest toward the end of a journey.

xíng chuán kào zhǎng duò, lǐ jiā kào jié yuē

行船靠掌舵, 理家靠节约。

行船靠掌舵, 理家靠節約。

Oarsmanship is vital to ship navigation as thrift is vital to managing a household.

xíng dòng shèng yú kōng tán

行动胜于空谈。

行動勝於空談。

Actions speak louder than words.

xíng yào hǎo bàn, zhù yào hǎo lín

行要好伴, 住要好邻。

行要好伴, 住要好鄰。

For a trip, choose good companions; for a home, choose good neighbors.

xíng yuǎn bì zì ěr, dēng gāo bì zì bēi

行远必自迩, 登高必自卑。

行遠必自邇, 登高必自卑。

To travel far, one must start near; to ascend to high places, one must begin from low places.

xiōng dì bù hé lín lǐ qī, jiàng xiàng bú mù lín guó qī

兄弟不和邻里欺, 将相不睦邻国欺。

兄弟不和鄰里欺, 將相不睦鄰國欺。

Brothers who can't get along will be bullied by neighbors; generals who can't get along will be attacked by neighboring countries.

xiōng dì bù hé yìng guò tiě

兄弟不和硬过铁。

兄弟不和硬過鐵。

Disharmony between brothers is tougher than iron.

xiōng dì xì yú qiáng, wài yù qí wǔ

兄弟阋于墙, 外御其侮。

兄弟鬩于牆, 外御其侮。

While brothers may quarrel at home, they will join forces against outside attacks.

xióng biàn shì yín, chén mò shì jīn

雄辩是银, 沉默是金。

雄辯是銀, 沉默是金。

Eloquence is silver, and silence is golden.

xiù cái bù chū mén, néng zhī tiān xià shì

秀才不出门, 能知天下事。

秀才不出門, 能知天下事。

The learned need not leave their homes to know what is going on in the world.

xiù cái è sǐ bú mài shū, zhuàng shì qióng sǐ bú mài yì

秀才饿死不卖书, 壮士穷死不卖艺。

秀才餓死不賣書, 壯士窮死不賣藝。

A scholar will not sell his books even when starving, and a warrior will not stoop to street performances.

xū xīn de rén xué shí dāng yī, jiāo ào de rén xué yī dāng shí

虚心的人学十当一，骄傲的人学一当十。

虛心的人學十當一，驕傲的人學一當十。

The humble feel they only have learned a little when they
have in fact studied a great deal, while the arrogant feel they
have learned a great deal when they have in fact studied only
a little.

xué bú yàn lǎo

学不厌老。

學不厭老。

One is never too old to learn.

xué bù zhī qiān, yì bì yǒu xiàn

学不知谦，艺必有限。

學不知謙，藝必有限。

Learning without modesty limits one's skills.

xué ěr bù sī zé wǎng, sī ěr bù xué zé dài

学而不思则罔，思而不学则殆。

學而不思則罔，思而不學則殆。

It is deceptive to study without reflection; it is dangerous to
reflect without studying.

xué pà yì zhī bàn jiě, fàn pà bàn shēng bù shóu

学怕一知半解，饭怕半生不熟。

學怕一知半解，飯怕半生不熟。

In study and in cooking, be concerned about half-baked results.

xué rú nì shuǐ xíng zhōu, bú jìn zé tuì

学如逆水行舟, 不进则退。

學如逆水行舟, 不進則退。

Learning is like paddling a canoe against the current - you will regress if you don't advance.

xué shàn sān nián, xué è yì zhāo

学善三年, 学恶一朝。

學善三年, 學惡一朝。

It takes three years to learn something good, but only a day to learn something bad.

xué wú lǎo shào, néng zhě wéi shī

学无老少, 能者为师。

學無老少, 能者為師。

In the area of learning, age make no difference, and those who know will be the teachers.

xué wú zhǐ jìng

学无止境。

學無止境。

There is no limit to learning.

xué xí rú gǎn lù, bù néng xiē yí bù

学习如赶路, 不能歇一步。

學習如趕路, 不能歇一步。

Learning is like an urgent journey, and you can't pause for even a moment.

xún xù jiàn jìn, wú yè bù chéng

循序渐进, 无业不成。

循序漸進, 無業不成。

Follow proper procedures and enjoy success in whatever you do.

Y

yán bì xìn, xíng bì guǒ
言必信, 行必果。
言必信, 行必果。
Promises must be kept and actions must be resolute.

yán duō bì shī
言多必失。
言多必失。
One is bound to have a slip of tongue if he talks too much.

yán shī chū gāo tú
严师出高徒。
嚴師出高徒。
A strict master produces a skilled apprentice.

yán shì ài, sōng shì hài, bù guǎn bú jiāo yào biàn huài
严是爱, 松是害, 不管不教要变坏。
嚴是愛, 鬆是害, 不管不教要變壞。
Strictness is love, leniency is harmful, and children will turn
bad without discipline and instruction.

yán shuāng jiàn zhēn mù

严霜见真木。

嚴霜見真木。

The best wood is found in harsh climates.

yán yǐ lǜ jǐ, kuān yǐ dài rén

严以律己，宽以待人。

嚴以律己，寬以待人。

Be strict with oneself and broad-minded toward others.

yǎn bú jiàn wéi jìng

眼不见为净。

眼不見為淨。

Out of sight, out of mind.

yǎn bú jiàn, xīn bù fán

眼不见，心不烦。

眼不見，心不煩。

Out of sight, out of mind.

yǎn xié xīn bú zhèng, bí wāi yì bù duān

眼斜心不正，鼻歪意不端。

眼斜心不正，鼻歪意不端。

Shifty eyes, shifty heart; crooked nose, crooked mind.

yáng máo chū zài yáng shēn shàng

羊毛出在羊身上。

羊毛出在羊身上。

Wool comes from sheep.

yǎng bīng qiān rì, yòng bīng yì shí

养兵千日, 用兵一时。

養兵千日, 用兵一時。

Train and maintain an army in peacetime in order to deploy it at a critical moment.

yǎng jūn rú yǎng hǔ, hǔ dà bì shāng rén

养军如养虎, 虎大必伤人。

養軍如養虎, 虎大必傷人。

Training soldiers is like training tigers; when the tiger is grown, it will injure others.

yǎng yào zì jǐ zhuā, hǎo yào bié rén kuā

痒要自己抓, 好要别人夸。

癢要自己抓, 好要別人誇。

Scratch your own itch, but let others praise your goodness.

yàng yàng tōng, yàng yàng sōng

样样通, 样样松

樣樣通, 樣樣鬆

Jack of all trades, master of none.

yǎo rén gǒu, bú lòu chǐ

咬人狗, 不露齿。

咬人狗, 不露齒。

The dog that bites won't bare its teeth.

yào bǔ bù rú shí bǔ

药补不如食补。

藥補不如食補。

Healthy food cures better than medicine.

yào bù néng yī jiǎ bìng, jiǔ bù néng jiě zhēn chóu

药不能医假病, 酒不能解真愁

藥不能醫假病, 酒不能解真愁

Medicine can not treat an imaginary illness and alcohol cannot solve real worries.

yào chī lóng ruò, zì jǐ xià hǎi

要吃龙肉, 自己下海。

要吃龍肉, 自己下海。

If you want to eat dragon meat, you'll have to go out and get it yourself.

yào zhī fù mǔ ēn, huái lǐ bào ér sūn

要知父母恩, 怀里抱儿孙。

要知父母恩, 懷裡抱兒孫。

You will understand a parent's love when you hold your own child in your arms.

yào zhī shān zhōng shì, xū wèn dǎ chái rén

要知山中事，须问打柴人。

要知山中事，須問打柴人。

If you want to know what is happening on the mountain, you must ask the firewood collector.

yào zhī xià shān lù, xū wèn guò lái rén

要知下山路，须问过来人。

要知下山路，須問過來人。

If you want to know how to get down off a mountain, you must ask the people who have done it.

yě huǒ shāo bú jìn, chūn fēng chuī yòu shēng

野火烧不尽，春风吹又生。

野火燒不盡，春風吹又生。

Not even a prairie fire can destroy the grass; it grows back when the spring breeze blows.

yè dào hèn míng yuè

夜盗恨明月。

夜盗恨明月。

Thieves in the night hate the moonlight.

yè jīng yú qín, huāng yú xī

业精于勤，荒于嬉。

業精于勤，荒于嬉。

In any undertaking, diligence leads to mastery while frivolity leads to decay.

yè yè fáng zéi bú shòu hài, tiān tiān fáng chóng bú shòu zāi

夜夜防贼不受害, 天天防虫不受灾。

夜夜防賊不受害, 天天防蟲不受災。

One will not be victimized if he guards against thieves night after night, and one will not suffer disasters if he guards against pests day after day.

yī shang cháng le bàn tuǐ, xīn yǎn duō le shòu lèi

衣裳长了绊腿, 心眼多了受累。

衣裳長了絆腿, 心眼多了受累。

Clothes that are too long will trip you as a mind that is full of unnecessary misgivings will vex you.

yī shí zú zé zhī róng rù

衣食足则知荣辱。

衣食足則知榮辱。

Honor and disgrace matter only to those who have fulfilled their material needs.

yí cùn guāng yīn yí cùn jīn, cùn jīn nán mǎi cùn guāng yīn

一寸光阴一寸金, 寸金难买寸光阴。

一寸光陰一寸金, 寸金難買寸光陰。

A moment of time is like a piece of gold, but a piece of gold won't buy a moment of time.

yí dài hǎo xí fù, sān dài hǎo ér sūn

一代好媳妇, 三代好儿孙。

一代好媳婦, 三代好兒孫。

One generation of good daughters-in-law produces three generations of good offspring.

yí dòng bù rú yí jìng

一动不如一静。

一動不如一靜。

When in doubt, better to stay put than to make a move.

yí rén mò yòng, yòng rén mò yí

疑人莫用，用人莫疑。

疑人莫用，用人莫疑。

Do not employ people you have doubts about, and do not
entertain doubts about the people you employ.

yí rén xīn bú zhèng, xīn zhèng bù yí rén

疑人心不正，心正不疑人。

疑人心不正，心正不疑人。

A suspicious person is not upright, and an upright person
has no suspicions.

yí rì dú shū yí rì gōng, yí rì bù dú shí rì kōng

一日读书一日功，一日不读十日空。

一日讀書一日功，一日不讀十日空。

A day of reading is a day of gain, and a day without reading is
ten days of loss.

yí rì shěng yì bǎ, sān nián mǎi pī mǎ

一日省一把，三年买匹马。

一日省一把，三年買匹馬。

Save a little every day, and you can buy a horse in three years.

yí wù xiáng yí wù

一物降一物。

一物降一物。

There is always one thing to subdue another.

yí xiào zhì bǎi bìng

一笑治百病。

一笑治百病。

Laughter is the medicine to cure one hundred illnesses.

yí xīn shēng àn guǐ

疑心生暗鬼。

疑心生暗鬼。

Suspicions create imaginary fears.

yí yàng mǐ, yǎng bǎi yàng rén

一样米，养百样人。

一樣米，養百樣人。

One kind of rice will nurture one hundred kinds of people.

yí yè fū qī bǎi rì ēn

一夜夫妻百日恩。

一夜夫妻百日恩。

One night as husband and wife, one hundred days of kindness.

yí yì bàng shēn, zhōng shēn shòu yòng
一艺傍身，终身受用。
一藝傍身，終身受用。
Possess a single skill, and reap the benefits your entire life.

yí zhāo bú shèn, mǎn pán jiē shū
一着不慎，满盘皆输。
一著不慎，滿盤皆輸。
One careless move leads to total loss.

yí zuì jiě qiān chóu, xǐng hòu hái zài chóu
一醉解千愁，醒后还在愁。
一醉解千愁，醒後還在愁。
Drink drowns your sorrow, but your sorrow returns the morning after.

yǐ shì fú rén kǒu, yǐ lǐ fú rén xīn
以势服人口，以理服人心。
以勢服人口，以理服人心。
Force may lead to agreement, but truth will lead to conviction.

yǐ yì bàng shēn, zhōng shēn shòu yòng
以艺傍身，终身受用。
以藝傍身，終身受用。
Possess a single skill, and reap the benefits your entire life.

yǐ yuàn bào yuàn shì yú, yǐ dé bào dé shì qíng

以怨报怨是愚, 以德报德是情。

以怨報怨是愚, 以德報德是情。

Repaying enmity with enmity shows stupidity while repaying kindness with kindness shows affection.

yì cháo tiān zǐ yì cháo chén

一朝天子一朝臣。

一朝天子一朝臣。

Every new sovereign brings his own courtiers.

yì ěr hǎo dǔ, zhòng mù nán yǎn

一耳好睹, 众目难掩。

一耳好睹, 眾目難掩。

You can plug one person's ears, but you can't close everyone's eyes.

yì fēn dù liàng yì fēn fú, néng rěn biàn shì yǒu fú rén

一分度量一分福, 能忍便是有福人。

一分度量一分福, 能忍便是有福人。

An ounce of tolerance, an ounce of good fortune.

yì fēn gēng yún, yì fēn shōu huò

一分耕耘, 一分收获。

一分耕耘, 一分收穫。

The more ploughing and weeding, the better the harvest.

yì fēn qián, yì fēn huò

一分钱, 一分货。

一分錢, 一分貨。

You get what you pay for.

yì gāo rén dǎn dà

艺高人胆大。

藝高人膽大。

Boldness of execution stems from superb skills.

yì ge bā zhǎng pāi bù xiǎng

一个巴掌拍不响。

一個巴掌拍不響。

A single hand cannot clap.

yì ge hǎo pí jiàng, méi yǒu hǎo xié yàng;
liǎng ge bèn pí jiàng, zuò shì hǎo shāng liáng

一个好皮匠, 没有好鞋样;两个笨皮匠, 做事好
商量。

一個好皮匠, 沒有好鞋樣;兩個笨皮匠, 做事好
商量。

One good shoemaker cannot come up with good shoe
patterns, but two clumsy shoemakers can consult with each
other.

Two heads are better than one.

yì ge hé shàng tiāo shuǐ hē, liǎng ge hé shàng tái shuǐ hē, sān ge hé shàng méi shuǐ hē

一个和尚挑水喝, 两个和尚抬水喝, 三个和尚没水喝。

一個和尚挑水喝, 兩個和尚抬水喝, 三個和尚沒水喝。

One monk carries water to drink, two monks lug water to drink, and three monks will have no water to drink.

Too many cooks spoil the soup.

yì ge wǎn bù xiǎng, liǎng ge wǎn dīng dāng

一个碗不响, 两个碗叮当。

一個碗不響, 兩個碗叮噹。

A single bowl makes no sound, but two bowls together will ring.

It takes two to tango.

yì gēn zhù zi dòng, gēn gēn wěi liáng yáo

一根柱子动, 根根尾梁摇。

一根柱子動, 根根尾樑搖。

The shifting of a single pillar will shake all of the beams.

yì huí shēng, èr huí shóu

一回生, 二回熟。

一回生, 二回熟。

First time strangers, second time friends.

yì jiā qì qiáng, liǎng jiā hǎo kàn

一家砌墙，两家好看。

一家砌牆，兩家好看。

When one family builds a wall, two families enjoy it.

yì jiā yǒu shì, sì lín bù ān

一家有事，四邻不安。

一家有事，四鄰不安。

Problems in one family produce grief for the whole neighborhood.

yì kǒu chī bù chéng ge pàng zi

一口吃不成个胖子。

一口吃不成個胖子。

Obesity is not the result of a single bite.

yì lǐ tōng, bǎi lǐ míng

一理通，百理明。

一理通，百理明。

Know one truth completely and understand all truths.

yì mǎ bú pèi liǎng ān, yì jiǎo nán tà liǎng chuán

一马不配两鞍，一脚难踏两船。

一馬不配兩鞍，一腳難踏兩船。

A horse is not fitted with two saddles and it is difficult for one leg to stand on two boats.

yì nián zhī jì zài yú chūn, yí rì zhī jì zài yú chén

一年之计在于春, 一日之计在于晨。

一年之計在於春, 一日之計在於晨。

The whole year's work depends on a good plan in the spring, and the whole day's work depends on a good start in the morning.

yì niǎo zì shǒu, shèng guò bǎi niǎo zài lín

一鸟在手, 胜过百鸟在林。

一鳥在手, 勝過百鳥在林。

A bird in the hand is better than two in the bush.

yì qín shēng bǎi qiǎo, yì lǎn shēng bǎi bìng

一勤生百巧, 一懒生百病。

一勤生百巧, 一懶生百病。

Diligence produces much ingenuity while laziness produces many illnesses.

yì qiú wú jià bǎo, nán dé yǒu qíng láng

易求无价宝, 难得有情郎。

易求無價寶, 難得有情郎。

It is easier to find a priceless treasure than to find an affectionate man.

yì quǎn fèi xíng, bǎi quǎn fèi shēng

一犬吠形, 百犬吠声。

一犬吠形, 百犬吠聲。

One dog barks at a shape, and one hundred dogs bark at the sound.

yì rén chuán xū, wàn rén chuán shí

一人传虚，万人传实。

一人傳虛，萬人傳實。

One man spreads a falsehood, and a multitude passes it
along as truth.

yì rén dé dào, jī quǎn shēng tiān

一人得道，鸡犬升天。

一人得道，雞犬升天。

When a man attains the Tao, even his pets ascend to heaven.
When a man gets to the top, his friends and relatives
accompany him there.

yì rén kāi jǐng, qiān jiā yǐn shuǐ

一人开井，千家饮水。

一人開井，千家飲水。

If one person builds a well, one thousand families will have
water to drink.

yì rén nán chèn bǎi rén yì

一人难称百人意。

一人難稱百人意。

You can't please everybody.

yì rén nán tiáo bǎi wèi gēng

一人难调百味羹。

一人難調百味羹。

You can't please everybody.

yì rén xiū lù, wàn rén ān bù

一人修路, 万人安步。

一人修路, 萬人安步。

One man builds a road, and ten thousand men can safely travel upon it.

yì rén zuò è, qiān rén zāo yāng

一人作恶, 千人遭殃。

一人作惡, 千人遭殃。

When one person performs a bad act, one thousand people suffer.

yì shān nán róng èr hǔ

一山难容二虎。

一山難容二虎。

One mountain cannot host two tigers.

yì shī zú chéng qiān gǔ hèn

一失足成千古恨。

一失足成千古恨。

One false step brings everlasting grief.

yì shí qiáng ruò zài yú lì, qiāng gǔ shèng fù zài yú lǐ

一时强弱在于力, 千古胜负在于理。

一時強弱在於力, 千古勝負在於理。

Temporary gain or loss its determined by your strength, but long-term victory or defeat is determined by your adherence to truth.

yì tiān bú liàn shǒu jiǎo màn, liǎng tiān bú liàn diū yí bàn

一天不练手脚慢, 两天不练丢一半。

一天不練手腳慢, 兩天不練丢一半。

Fail to practice one day and your skills will fall behind, but fail to practice two days and your skills will be gone.

yì xīn bù néng èr yòng

一心不能二用。

一心不能二用。

One mind cannot be put to two uses.

yì yán jì chū, sì mǎ nán zhuī

一言既出, 驷马难追。

一言既出, 駟馬難追。

A word once spoken can't be retrieved even by a team of horses.

yì zhāo bèi shé yǎo, shí nián pà cǎo shéng

一朝被蛇咬, 十年怕草绳。

一朝被蛇咬, 十年怕草繩。

Once bitten by a snake, one shies away from coiled rope for the next ten years.

yì zhēn bù bǔ, qiān zhēn nán féng

一针不补, 千针难缝。

一針不補, 千針難縫。

A stitch in time saves nine.

yì zhēng liǎng chǒu, yí ràng liǎng yǒu

一争两丑, 一让两有。

一爭兩醜, 一讓兩有。

One fight sullies two persons, and one compromise benefits two persons.

yì zhī zhēn wú liǎng tóu lì

一枝针无两头利。

一枝針無兩頭利。

A single needle has only one point.

yì zhú èr tú, yí tù bù dé

一逐二兔, 一兔不得。

一逐二兔, 一兔不得。

If you chase after two rabbits, you'll catch neither.

yīn yuán kě yù bù kě qiú

姻缘可遇不可求。

姻緣可遇不可求。

Marital bliss arises spontaneously, and it can't be sought after.

yīn yuán tiān zhù dìng

姻缘天注定。

姻緣天註定。

Marital bliss is predetermined by Heaven.

yǐn shuǐ yào sī yuán, wéi rén bú wàng běn
饮水要思源，为人不忘本。
飲水要思源，為人不忘本。
When drinking water, think of the source; when living your
life, remember who you are.

yīng xióng bú pà chū shēn dī
英雄不怕出身低。
英雄不怕出身低。
Humble origins trouble not the hero.

yīng xióng nán dí bìng lái mó
英雄难敌病来磨
英雄難敵病來磨
Even a hero cannot withstand the suffering of illness.

yīng xióng nán guò měi rén guān
英雄难过美人关。
英雄難過美人關。
Even heroes find it hard to resist beauty.

yīng xióng suǒ jiàn lüè tóng
英雄所见略同。
英雄所見略同。
Great minds think alike.

yīng xióng yǒu lèi bù qīng tán

英雄有泪不轻弹。

英雄有淚不輕彈。

Heroes fight back their tears.

yōng rén duō hòu fú

庸人多厚福。

庸人多厚福。

Fortune favors fools.

yòng rén qián cái, tì rén xiāo zāi

用人钱财, 替人消灾。

用人錢財, 替人消災。

If you use someone's money, you must help him ward off disaster.

yóu jiǎn rù shē yì, yóu shē rù jiǎn nán

由俭入奢易, 由奢入俭难。

由儉入奢易, 由奢入儉難。

It is easy to go from frugality to extravagance, but hard to go from extravagance to frugality.

yǒu bìng cái zhī jiàn shì xiān

有病才知健是仙。

有病才知健是仙。

Health is not valued until illness comes.

yǒu bìng zǎo zhì, shěng qián shěng shì

有病早治，省钱省事。

有病早治，省錢省事。

Tend to an illness early, and it will save you both money and effort.

yǒu fú bù kě xiǎng jìn, yǒu huà bù kě shuō jué

有福不可享尽，有话不可说绝。

有福不可享盡，有話不可說絕。

Don't enjoy all of your wealth and don't issue ultimatums.

yǒu héng chǎn, bù rú yǒu héng xīn

有恒产，不如有恒心。

有恆產，不如有恆心。

Better to have vast perseverance than a vast estate.

yǒu jiè yǒu huán, zài jiè bù nán

有借有还，再借不难。

有借有還，再借不難。

Return what you have borrowed and you may borrow again.

yǒu lǐ bú pà shì lái yā, rén zhèng bú pà yǐng zi xié

有理不怕势来压，人正不怕影子歪。

有理不怕勢來壓，人正不怕影子歪。

Those who are in the right are not concerned about being intimidated by force, and those who are upright are not concerned about their shadows being crooked.

yǒu lǐ bú zài shēng gāo

有理不在声高。

有理不在聲高。

Truth is not determined by the loudness of the voice.

yǒu lǐ zǒu biàn tiān xià, wú lǐ cùn bù nán xíng

有理走遍天下, 无理寸步难行。

有理走遍天下, 無理寸步難行。

When you are in the right, you can go anywhere; when you are in the wrong, you can go nowhere.

yǒu mā de hái zi xiàng ge bǎo, méi niáng de hái zi xiàng gēn cǎo

有妈的孩子像个宝, 没娘的孩子像根草。

有媽的孩子像個寶, 沒娘的孩子像根草。

A child with a mother is like a treasure, and a child without a mother is like a lone blade of grass.

yǒu qí fù bì yǒu qí zǐ

有其父必有其子。

有其父必有其子。

Like father, like son.

yǒu qián bàn shì chèn xīn yì

有钱办事称心意。

有錢辦事稱心意。

Money helps you get your way.

yǒu qián cháng xiǎng wú qián rì, fēng nián cháng jì dà huāng nián

有钱常想无钱日，丰年常记大荒年。

有錢常想無錢日，豐年常記大荒年。

Think of days of poverty when you have money, and remember the lean years when reaping a rich harvest.

yǒu qián gài bǎi chǒu

有钱盖百丑。

有錢蓋百醜。

Money conceals ugliness.

yǒu qián nán mǎi hòu huǐ yào

有钱难买后悔药。

有錢難買後悔藥。

No amount of money can buy medicine to treat regrets.

yǒu qián nán mǎi shào nián shí

有钱难买少年时。

有錢難買少年時。

Money cannot buy back your youth.

yǒu qián néng shǐ guǐ tuī mò

有钱能使鬼推磨。

有錢能使鬼推磨。

With money, you can make the ghost work the mill.

yǒu qián rén pà shì

有钱人怕事。

有錢人怕事。

The rich fear trouble.

yǒu qián yì tiáo lóng, wú qián yì tiáo chóng

有钱一条龙, 无钱一条虫。

有錢一條龍, 無錢一條蟲。

When you are rich, you are treated like a dragon; when you are poor, you are treated like a worm.

yǒu shān bì yǒu lù, yǒu shuǐ bì yǒu dù

有山必有路, 有水比有渡。

有山必有路, 有水比有渡。

Where there is a mountain, there is a pass; where there is water, there is a ferry.

yǒu shàng bú qù de tiān, méi yǒu guò bú qù de guān

有上不去的天, 没有过不去的关。

有上不去的天, 沒有過不去的關。

There may be heights that cannot be scaled, but there are no barriers that can't be broken.

yǒu yí lì, bì yǒu yí bì

有一利, 必有一弊。

有一利, 必有一弊。

Where there is a pro, there is a con.

yǒu yuán qiān lǐ lái xiāng huì, wú yuán duì miàn bù xiāng shì

有缘千里来相会, 无缘对面不相识。

有緣千里來相會, 無緣對面不相識。

Fate will bring two people together though they are separated by one thousand miles; fate will prevent two people from meeting though they are standing face to face.

yǒu zhì bú zài nián gāo

有志不在年高。

有志不在年高。

With ambition, age matters not.

yǒu zhì fù rén shèng guò nán zǐ

有志妇人胜过男子。

有志婦人勝過男子。

Women with ambition are more capable than men.

yǒu zhì piāo yáng guò hǎi, wú zhì cùn bù nán xíng

有志飘洋过海, 无志寸步难行。

有志飄洋過海, 無志寸步難行。

With aspirations, you can go anywhere, and without aspirations, you can go nowhere.

yǒu zhì zhě shì jìng chéng

有志者事竟成。

有志者事竟成。

Where there is a will, there is a way.

yòu yào mǎ ér pǎo de kuài, yòu yào mǎ ér bù chī cǎo

又要马儿跑得快, 又要马儿不吃草。

又要馬兒跑得快, 又要馬兒不吃草。

You can't expect the horse to run fast if you don't let it graze.

yú bàng xiāng zhēng, yú wēng dé lì

鹬蚌相争, 渔翁得利。

鷸蚌相爭, 漁翁得利。

When the snipe and the clam fight, the fisherman benefits.

yú zhě qiān yǔ, bì yǒu yì dé

愚者千虑, 必有一得。

愚者千慮, 必有一得。

Over time, even the fool will occasionally hit on a good idea.

yǔ bù néng xià yì nián, rén bù néng qióng yí bèi

雨不能下一年, 人不能穷一辈。

雨不能下一年, 人不能窮一輩。

Rain will not fall all year long, and people will not be poor throughout their lives.

yǔ rén fāng biàn, zì jǐ fāng biàn

予人方便, 自己方便。

予人方便, 自己方便。

Doing someone a favor is tantamount to doing yourself a favor.

yù bù zhuó, bù chéng qì

玉不琢, 不成器。

玉不琢, 不成器。

If jade is not cut and polished, it can't be made into anything.

yù fáng shèng yú zhì liáo

预防胜于治疗。

預防勝於治療。

Prevention is better than cure.

yù qióng qiān lǐ mù, gèng shàng yì céng lóu

欲穷千里目, 更上一层楼。

欲窮千里目, 更上一層樓。

If you want to see farther, you have to go higher.

yù sù zé bù dá

欲速则不达。

欲速則不達。

Haste makes waste.

yù yuǎn shì fēi, shèn jiāo wéi xiān

欲远是非, 慎交为先。

欲遠是非, 慎交為先。

Choose your friends carefully if you want to stay out of trouble.

yù zhī xīn fù shì, xiān tīng kǒu zhōng yán

欲知心腹事，先听口中言。

欲知心腹事，先聽口中言。

If you wish to know what is in a person's heart, listen first to what he says.

yuān chóu yí jiě bù yí jié

冤仇宜解不宜结。

冤仇宜解不宜結。

Better to resolve enmity than to create it.

yuān jiā lù zhǎi

冤家路窄。

冤家路窄。

One can't avoid one's enemy.

yuān yǒu tóu, zhài yǒu zhǔ

冤有头，债有主。

冤有頭，債有主。

Put the saddle on the right horse.

yuǎn chù zhuó yǎn, jìn chù zhuó shǒu

远处着眼，近处着手。

遠處著眼，近處著手。

Set long-term goals, but work on short-term tasks.

yuǎn qīn bù rú jìn lín

远亲不如近邻。

遠親不如近鄰。

Neighbors are dearer than distant relatives.

yuǎn shuǐ bù jiě jìn kě

远水不解近渴。

遠水不解近渴。

Distant water won't quench immediate thirst.

A slow remedy cannot meet an urgency.

yuǎn shuǐ jiù bù liǎo jìn huǒ

远水救不了近火。

遠水救不了近火。

Distant water won't put out a fire close at hand.

A slow remedy cannot meet an urgency.

yuǎn zhù xiāng, jìn zhù liáng

远住香, 近住凉。

遠住香, 近住涼。

Live near and be far from the heart, live far away and be near to the heart.

yuàn zi lǐ pǎo bù chū qiān lǐ mǎ

院子里跑不出千里马。

院子裡跑不出千里馬。

A strong steed cannot be raised in the yard.

yuè ér wān wān zhào jiǔ zhōu, jǐ jiā huān lè jǐ jiā chóu

月儿弯弯照九州，几家欢乐几家愁。

月兒彎彎照九州，幾家歡樂幾家愁。

When the crescent moon shines over China, some families are happy and other are sad.

yún bú jù jí yǔ bú xià, rén bù tuán jié lì bú dà

云不聚集雨不下，人不团结力不大。

雲不聚集雨不下，人不團結力不大。

If the clouds don't form, there will be no rain; if people don't unite, they will have no power.

Z

zǎo shuì zǎo qǐ jīng shén hǎo

早睡早起精神好。

早睡早起精神好。

Early to bed and early to rise makes a man full of vitality.

zhǎn cǎo bù chú gēn, chūn fēng chuī yòu shēng

斩草不除根, 春风吹又生。

斬草不除根, 春風吹又生。

If you don't pull the root out when you weed, the problem will return when the spring comes.

zhè shān wàng zhe nà shān gāo

这山望着那山高。

這山望著那山高。

The grass is always greener on the other side of the fence.

zhēn jīn bú pà huǒ liàn

真金不怕火炼。

真金不怕火煉。

Genuine gold fears no fire.

zhēn lǐ yù biàn yù míng

真理愈辩愈明。

真理愈辯愈明。

Truth emerges from vigorous debate.

zhèng dàn hǎo tiāo, piān dàn nán ái

正担好挑, 偏担难挨。

正擔好挑, 偏擔難挨。

The pole is easy to carry if the load is balanced.

zhèng qì gāo, xié qì xiāo

正气高, 邪气消。

正氣高, 邪氣消。

A healthy atmosphere drives away evil.

zhī jǐ zhī bǐ, bǎi zhàn bǎi shèng

知己知彼, 百战百胜。

知己知彼, 百戰百勝。

Knowing both oneself and one's opponent is the certain way to victory.

zhī shì jiù shì lì liàng

知识就是力量。

知識就是力量。

Knowledge is power.

zhī shì yù qiǎn, zì xìn yù shēn

知识愈浅，自信愈深。

知識愈淺，自信愈深。

The more shallow the knowledge, the greater the arrogance.

zhī zhě bù yán, yán zhě bù zhī

知者不言，言者不知。

知者不言，言者不知。

Those who know do not talk, and those who talk do not know.

zhī zhū qín zhī wǎng, zǒng yǒu fēi lái chóng

蜘蛛勤织网，总有飞来虫。

蜘蛛勤織網，總有飛來蟲。

If a spider works hard spinning webs, it will eventually catch insects.

zhī zhū zhāng wǎng hǎo tiān qì

蜘蛛张网好天气。

蜘蛛張網好天氣。

Spider webs portend fine weather.

zhī zú cháng lè

知足常乐。

知足常樂。

A contented mind is a perpetual feast.

zhǐ bāo bú zhù huǒ

纸包不住火。

紙包不住火。

You can't wrap fire in paper.

Truth will out.

zhǐ gěi jūn zǐ kàn mén, bù gěi xiǎo rén dāng jiā

只给君子看门, 不给小人当家。

只給君子看門, 不給小人當家。

Better to be the doorman for a gentleman than the manager
for a scoundrel.

zhǐ qín méi jiǎn, hǎo bǐ yǒu zhēn méi xiàn

只勤没俭, 好比有针没线。

只勤沒儉, 好比有針沒線。

Diligence without frugality is like a needle without thread.

zhǐ yào gōng fū shēn, tiě chǔ mó chéng zhēn

只要功夫深, 铁杵磨成针。

只要功夫深, 鐵杵磨成針。

If you work at it hard enough, you can grind an iron rod
down to a needle.

zhǐ yào kǔ gàn, shì chéng yí bàn

只要苦干, 事成一半。

只要苦幹, 事成一半。

Work hard and the job is half done.

zhì fú měng hǔ fēi yīng xióng, yì zhù pí qì zhēn hǎo hàn

制服猛虎非英雄, 抑住脾气真好汉。

制服猛虎非英雄, 抑住脾氣真好漢。

The true hero is not one who can subdue a vicious tiger, but rather, he is one who can curb his own temper.

zhì zhě kuǎ yán, yú zhě duō zuǐ

智者寡言, 愚者多嘴。

智者寡言, 愚者多嘴。

The wise say little while fools babble.

zhì zhě qiān lǜ, bì yǒu yì shī

智者千虑, 必有一失。

智者千慮, 必有一失。

Even the greatest men stumble.

zhòng guā dé guā, zhòng dòu dé dòu

种瓜得瓜, 种豆得豆。

種瓜得瓜, 種豆得豆。

As you sow, so shall you reap.

zhòng kǒu nán tiáo

众口难调。

眾口難調。

You can't please all of the people all of the time.

zhòng qíng yì jǔ, dú lì nán chéng

众擎易举, 独力难成。

眾擎易舉, 獨力難成。

It's easy to lift a load with many people, but it is hard to do it alone.

zhòng shǎng zhī xià, bì yǒu yǒng fū

重赏之下, 必有勇夫。

重賞之下, 必有勇夫。

When a considerable reward is offered, brave fellows are bound to step forward.

zhòng wéi qīng gēn

重为轻根。

重為輕根。

Heaviness is the root of lightness.

zhū duō ròu jiàn

猪多肉贱。

豬多肉賤。

When pigs are plenty, pork is cheap.

zhù rén wéi kuài lè zhī běn

助人为快乐之本。

助人為快樂之本。

Helping others is the foundation of happiness.

zhuō yú yào xià shuǐ, fá mù yào rù lín

抓鱼要下水, 伐木要入林。

抓魚要下水, 伐木要入林。

You have to go to sea to catch fish, and you have to go to the forest to cut wood.

zì jǐ dié dǎo zì jǐ pá

自己跌倒自己爬。

自己跌倒自己爬。

If you fall down on your own, get up on your own.

zì jiā de wén zhāng, rén jiā de pó niáng

自家的文章, 人家的婆娘。

自家的文章, 人家的婆娘。

In writing, one's own work is better; in women, the other man's is better.

zòng ér hài ér, zòng qī hài zì jǐ

纵儿害儿, 纵妻害自己。

縱兒害兒, 縱妻害自己。

Spoil your child, harm your child; spoil your wife, harm yourself.

zǒu jìn qí qū lù, zì yǒu píng tǎn tú

走尽崎岖路, 自有平坦途。

走盡崎嶇路, 自有平坦途。

After a rough road comes a smooth path.

zuǐ qiǎo duó shàng fēng

嘴巧夺上风。

嘴巧奪上風。

The eloquent are at an advantage.

zuǐ shàng wú máo, bàn shì bù láo

嘴上无毛, 办事不牢。

嘴上無毛, 辦事不牢。

A man who is too young to grow a beard is not dependable.

zuò chī shān kōng

坐吃山空。

坐吃山空。

Sit idle and eat, and in time, your whole fortune will be used up.

zuò shì bù yī zhòng, lèi sǐ yě wú gōng

做事不依众, 累死也无功。

做事不依眾, 累死也無功。

No matter how hard you work, you won't get credit if you don't' comply with the public.

zuò shì róng yì zuò rén nán

做事容易做人难。

做事容易做人難。

It's easy to do a job but difficult to conduct oneself properly.

zuò yì háng, yuàn yì háng, dào lǎo bú zài háng

做一行，怨一行，到老不在行。

做一行，怨一行，到老不在行。

Grumble about your profession and you'll be good at nothing when you get old.

zuò yí rì hé shàng, zhuàng yí rì zhōng

做一日和尚，撞一日钟。

做一日和尚，撞一日鐘。

If you're a monk for a day, toll the bell for a day.
Carry out the duties of your station.

English Key Word Index

The English key word index contains an alphabetical listing of English key words, by which is meant the English words most closely associated with the meaning and significance of the proverb. All numbers refer to page numbers.

Chinese Character Concordance

Entries are Chinese characters most closely associated with the meaning and significance of a given proverb. In most cases, the Chinese characters correspond directly to the English key words for a given proverb. The entries are arranged based on pinyin alphabetical spelling for the characters. All numbers refer to page numbers.

A
哀 1, 101
矮 126
爱(愛) 1, 11, 25, 161
鞍 88, 120, 187
岸 78

B
百 2, 3
败(敗) 31, 102, 136, 137, 169
搬 89
伴 170
宝(寶) 19, 66, 85, 128, 188
饱(飽) 3
报(報) 132
豹 3
笨 17, 185
崩 23
比 115
毕(畢) 70
弊 49

变(變) 102, 112
辩(辯) 171
别 162
兵 5, 6, 22, 54, 177
病 6, 8, 63, 72, 138, 168, 193, 194, 195
卑 170
悲 4, 133
波 144
薄 56
不 150

C
财(財) 13, 15, 22, 46, 56, 108, 123, 160, 163
操 15
草 6
差 16
茶 49, 96
柴 11, 28, 87, 117
昌 62

石 46
时(時)138
食 46, 58, 92, 103, 137
实(實)35, 104
事 12, 45, 49, 50, 53, 140, 187
识(識)143, 206, 207
是 139
试(試)51
势(勢)195
收 38, 162, 184
手 108, 109, 140
瘦 85
寿(壽)109, 146
书(書)10, 54, 101, 171
疏 2
输(輸)183
鼠 55, 80, 93
树(樹)27, 91, 138, 142, 143,
　　165
速 6
水 53, 78, 86, 100, 203
说(說)59
私 145, 154
思 6, 17
丝(絲)28
湿(濕)13
死 1, 3, 97
俗 20
随(隨)66
岁月(歲月)45
孙(孫)89, 180

T
台(臺)73
贪(貪)13, 147, 160
谈(談)170
甜 11
天 20, 59, 93, 148, 149, 151,
　　192
调(調)189, 209
铁(鐵)26, 82, 84, 134, 171
听(聽)13, 59, 66, 139, 151
桶 78
途 132
土 73, 155, 169
头(頭)45, 126
兔 153, 192
团(團)139, 151, 153
吞 124

W
瓦 42
歪 195
外 154
碗 186
网(網)207
危 85
为(為)129
闻(聞)3
稳(穩)157
问(問)4, 14, 17, 100, 157
屋 90
悟 107